LETTERS
to PRIESTS

Blessings

Josette

LETTERS
to PRIESTS

JOANNE MCKENNA

TATE PUBLISHING *& Enterprises*

Published by Tate Publishing & Enterprises, LLC
127 E. Trade Center Terrace | Mustang, Oklahoma 73064 USA
1.888.361.9473 | www.tatepublishing.com

Tate Publishing is committed to excellence in the publishing industry. The company reflects the philosophy established by the founders, based on Psalm 68:11,
"The Lord gave the word and great was the company of those who published it."

Book design copyright © 2010 by Tate Publishing, LLC. All rights reserved.
Cover design by Kellie Southerland
Interior design by Scott Parrish
Photo by Timothy Datchuck

Published in the United States of America

ISBN: 978-1-61663-875-7
Religion / Meditations
10.08.09

Dedication

I would like to dedicate this book to the late Dolores Suriani and to all priests who provide support and guidance in the spiritual life every day. This book is a tribute to priests, deacons, ministers, and all who have responded to God's call to "love and serve" (Deuteronomy 10:12).

In remembrance of Dennis, who recently took his life in despair. May our continued prayer lift the hearts of those who are most in need of hope.

Acknowledgments

No book is ever the product of one person's efforts, and this one is certainly no different. For myself, I am indebted to my family and friends, who are the moral fiber behind these pages; especially my deceased parents who passed on their faith, dedication to family values, and taught me unconditional love; as well as my husband, James, for his constant love and support, without which this would not be possible. To his sons Todd and Kyle: thank you for allowing me to share your parents' pride and love, which extends to the entire McKenna clan whose generosity epitomizes the true meaning of family.

I would like to thank my beautiful daughter, Melissa, the *sunshine* of my life; and Carlos, who is like a son to me. I am grateful to my grand-children (who have no concept of old) for their understanding of time-out from indulging them. The spirited and talented Justice, of whom I am extremely proud; for like her mother, is an exam-ple of courage and perseverance; Alyssa, with her ever-present smile who is always there with a hug; the twins, Zion and Zachai, for their imagi-nation and the joy they bring us all.

I am eternally grateful as well to my four wonderful sisters. Audrey, who is my life-line, my phone call, and my audience participation all rolled up in one giving heart; for Patty and Bill, a more genuine, selfless couple I will never know; Sandra, the matriarch of this wonderful Ital-ian family, who is the eldest and the wisest in so many ways; Timi-Ann, who gives her all, and then some, to everything she does with Marie, Kaleigh, and Maggie, her warm and wonderful family.

I would like to thank my nieces and neph-ews; Elizabeth Ferri, for her research assistance along with Timothy Datchuck for his talent in photography.

To Stephanie, for her wit and her charm, and her son Nicholas; Tiffany, whom I adore, and her daughter, Atalysse, the newest family member and the most precious of all.

To Bobby, Buddy, and Tommy, my brothers-in-law, who were taken from us much too soon. We miss them so very much.

I am indebted to Paula Hillman for her friendship, her prayer, her generous gift of time, and her trust in the triune God. Her contributions in the final stages were invaluable. Thanks to Fritzi and of course, Mollie. I am equally beholding to Rhonda Fougere whose challenge prompted the compilation of this work.

For over twenty years I have been gifted by the dedicated staff of Adcare hospital, including the Dr. Ronald Pike and David Hillis families, the nurses and counselors, who have devoted their lives to the care of patients and families suffering from the disease of addiction. I am grateful to all who have entrusted me with the privilege of sharing in the work of recovery.

Other contributions to this most important endeavor include the many groups who have supported me in the spiritual life. The teachers of the Insight Meditation Society and many parish and monastic communities have provided limitless refuge and silence for which I will be forever grateful.

In conclusion, I would never have begun this wonderful journey with the living God without the spiritual direction of many devoted and tireless priests and religious. The depth of my gratitude to these men and women is unspeakable.

To Father Raymond Suriani and his sister, Donna; thank you for sharing your mother with God, his church, and his anointed ones throughout your life.

I would be remiss if I did not recognize the people at Tate publishing whose dedication and service in Christ's name made this endeavor possible.

"Give thanks to God, Bless his name; good indeed is the lord, whose love endures, whose faithfulness lasts through every age" (Psalm 100:4–5).

In the name of the Father and the Son and the Holy Spirit.

Amen.

Table of Contents

Penitence

Priesthood

Part II

Preface

Letters to Priests is a compilation of letters, prayers, and excerpts written in honor of those who daily offer their lives in service to the Lord. They are intended to provide inspiration, hope, and encouragement for priests and pastors who strive for spiritual perfection in a world sorely in need of support and understanding.

What a more appropriate time than now to join the millions who have united with his holiness Benedict XVI who has established a special year for priests from June 19, 2009–June 10, 2010. This declaration coincides with the 150th anniversary of St. John Vianney, patron of priests. The focus, exclaims the pontiff, is to "encourage priests in the striving for spiritual perfection on which, above all, the effectiveness of their ministry depends." [1]

Prologue

If there exists some wonderment about how a laywoman became so interested in a mission of prayer for priests, I would say, as well there should be. That is, I would, if it did not begin with a saint of a woman placed in my life at a very early age. Dolores Suriani, a mother of two young children at the time, was the parish "secretary." She was the kind of secretary who peppered her all-important duties amidst prayer, spiritual direction, and healing. Yes, Dolores had a magnificent gift! Every priest she encountered knew it. Many came to her regularly, others queried from afar, but none could ignore that this simple, spiritual guide was blessed.

I was an adolescent at the time, young enough to have "a beginner's mind" and old enough to lack solid direction. It was a perfect opportunity to capture added energy for the intention of priests everywhere. Dolores was guided by her relationship with Mary. I was never quite sure what that was, but I knew that when she spoke I should listen and follow. There was something much bigger than I at stake, and I did not need to know more than that. Now, I am not one who typically accepts unreservedly then acts accordingly, but during these years it seemed perfectly natural.

Prayer was solicited with earnest from anyone and everyone who would listen. Groups formed to pray for priests and hundreds of prayer cards printed and distributed of Saint John Vianney with "A Prayer for Priests" on the back.

Hence, this work began. It was 1966. The climate in the church was quite a bit different then, but it is said that "the more things change, the more they stay the same," and priesthood is no exception. The call to "serve the Lord in sincerity and truth" (Joshua 24:14) bears many of the same sorrows and joy in any age, and I pray with the generous use of Scripture, literature, the mothers and fathers of the church—lay, religious, and ordained alike—you will find support and comfort in the following letters that were written over the years with this intention.

By his grace, I pray you find tucked between these lines some connection with your own journey, which reassures you that you are not alone and refresh in you the breath of God. This is the sole purpose of this work.

May God who has begun this great work in us all bring it to completion. Amen.

Saint John Vianney

by Ade Bethune[2]
St. Jean-Baptiste-Marie Vianney

Curé of Ars, born at Dardilly, near
Lyons, France, on May 8, 1786; died at
Ars, August 4, 1859. (Biography App 1)

Prayer for Priests

O Jesus, our great high priest,
Hear my humble prayers on behalf
  of your priest, Father [N].
Give him a deep faith

a bright and firm hope
and a burning love
which will ever increase
in the course of his priestly life.

In his loneliness, comfort him
In his sorrows, strengthen him
In his frustrations, point out to him

that it is through suffering that the soul is purified,
and show him that he is
  needed by the Church,
he is needed by souls,
he is needed for the work of redemption.
O loving Mother Mary, Mother of Priests,

take to your heart your son
  who is close to you
because of his priestly ordination,
and because of the power
  which he has received
to carry on the work of Christ
in a world which needs him so much.

Be his comfort, be his joy, be his strength,

and especially help him
to live and to defend the ideals of
  consecrated celibacy. Amen

John Joseph, Cardinal Carberry (+1998)
  Archbishop of St. Louis 1968–1979 [3]

Icon of Ministerial Priesthood

by Monsignor Anthony LaFemina

"There is one God, and there is one mediator between God and men, the man Christ Jesus, who gave Himself as a ransom for all."

1Timothy 2:5

God our Father, you reveal your omnipotence in the superabundance of your mercy, poured forth into the world through the sacred wounds of your Son and our Redeemer.

We ardently pray that your sacred ministers may be clear reflections of your mercy. May they, with every word and deed of their life, illumine humanity, disoriented by sin, and bring it back to you, who are love.

We ask this, Father, through your Son, our Lord Jesus Christ, who lives and reigns with you in the unity of the Holy Spirit, forever and ever. Amen[4]

—Monsignor LaFemina

Innocence

Beginning

Beginnings of all kinds seem to share a sense of innocence and simplicity. The journey to priesthood is no different. At the core, lies the culmination of a lifetime of experience in which longing becomes realized and life is transformed. We begin, as on that most holy day, *in remembrance* of such joy.

Dear Father,

It is the mass of the Lord's Supper! Today you have been given the wondrous and mysterious gift of Christ himself. Simple and magnificent is the gift of priesthood. In community, we offer praise and thanksgiving.

It is Maundy Thursday, and we are witness to God's gift to man and man's gift to God.[5]

May he guide your every step as you draw nearer, and when this awe-inspiring mystery feels more daunting than comforting, remember the call of the first disciples.[6] Recall the healings that followed.

> "The Lord has sworn (an oath) and will not change his mind (Hebrews 7: 21).

> "You are a priest forever according to the order of Melchizedek" (Hebrews 7: 17)

> The small light—simple, transparent light—visible and invisible, beckons us to come.[7]

Dear Father,

There is story about a Christian hermit in the desert of Egypt.

It seems that a young aspirant once came to visit the hermitage of a holy man, who was sitting in the doorway of his quarters at sunset. The old man's dog stretched out across the threshold. The spiritual seeker presented this problem. Why is it, Abba, that some who seek God come to the desert and are zealous in prayer but leave after one year, while others remain faithful to the quest for a lifetime?

The old man smiled and replied, "Let me tell you a story. One day I was sitting here quietly in the sun with my dog. Suddenly a large, white rabbit ran across in front of us. My dog jumped up barking loudly and took off after that big rabbit. He chased the rabbit over the hills with a passion. Soon other dogs joined him, attracted by his barking. What a sight it was as the pack of dogs ran barking across the creeks, up stony embankments, through thickets and thorns. Gradually, however, one by one the other dogs dropped out of the pursuit, discouraged by the course and frustrated by the chase. Only my dog continued to hotly pursue the white rabbit. In that story, young man, is the answer to your question."

The young man sat confused in silence. Finally, he said, "Abba, I don't understand. What is the connection between the rabbit chase and the quest for holiness?"

"You fail to understand", answered the hermit, "because you failed to ask the obvious question. Why didn't the other dogs continue the chase? They had not seen the rabbit. Unless you see your prey, the chase is just too difficult. You will

lack the determination and passion necessary to keep up the pursuit".[8]

You are here because you have experienced
the divine mystery.

You have seen the rabbit.

✝

Dear Father,

This is the proof that we remain in him and he in us. We see his face reflected in the whole of creation. We surrender, and in discovering his will, we give him glory. In the sacrament of each moment, in quiet awareness, we stand with his disciples and pray. We have seen for ourselves and can testify that the father has sent his son as savior of the world, and he is as close to you as you are to your very self.

Beyond imagination and reason, is he. So we leave what is known; hearing do not be afraid, come and see. By his grace alone we proclaim our own fiat. Just look and listen and rest in his grace, rest in him the sole master.

Father, I pray each day for your intention with constant intercession to our lady, mother of priests, to cover you with her mantle of peace as only a mother can. By virtue of your priest-hood, you will forever be in her constant care and protection. May she guide you to her son's most sacred heart in the depths of your own.

> "The greatest treasure of the universe is that we shall find what we seek."
>
> —Lao Tsu[9]

✝

Dear Father,

St. Benedict said, "Instructed with learned ignorance, furnished with unlearned wisdom under the guidance of the Holy Spirit who knows where this journey will lead you?"[10]

We pray it leads to the glory of God, recognizing that there are many paths; not the least of which includes contemplative prayer and Eastern meditation. Father Merton's life ended at the juncture of just such an exploration into *unlearned* wisdom, but not before he discovered, God is … *all in all.*

Father, touch what is most sacred within you. Listen to him who loves you and with yourself be gentle and patient without judgment or expectation. I lift you each day before him who will protect, guide, and strengthen you in the months ahead with a peace that the world cannot give.

> "I have a hole in my shoe from where I've
> walked on a rainbow and a rip in my shirt

from where I've hung from a star and after traveling the universe for more than a million years now ... "[11]

I've discovered that the freedom to dance, perhaps to suffer, but to take that chance is well worth the struggle.

✝

Dear Father,

You have truly been an instrument of God's healing peace in the world. The Lord Jesus Christ is the son of the living God and your humble response to his call has brought about the lived reality of his presence.

Father, you have served as a source of strength and support for many. As his will, his promise, and his plan unfold ever so slowly, he continues to bless your priesthood as you serve him, heart filled with gladness (cf. Psalm 4: 7).

We will continue to pray for you as always. Peace be with you and all who have been given the gift of his anointing from throughout the ages.

> "Jesus the Jew, peddler of choices, and fisher for God. Let him pass." [12]

Growing

The pathway to glory is a long road it seems, and we're living our lives in between. It is in-between that the glory of God unfolds gradually. The challenge is to travel the *middle path*. Celebrate this day as if it were your last day, pray as if it were your only day to offer praise and thanksgiving.

Dear Father,

Recall the words spoken to you on the day that you received the gifts from the people. The invitation goes deeper than ritual. It brings about a death that results from a gradual triumph of the power of Christ in the midst of weakness (II Cor. 4:12). It is quiet and unassuming. There is little glory in these moments, usually alone and unshared, because these are triumphs for which there are few, if any, words.

In the spirit of love and prayer, know the company of saints is with you. Be strengthened by their lives and their courage. Take the time and space you need and be at peace.

> "I learn it daily, learn it with pain to which
> I am grateful: patience is everything." [13]
> —Rainer Maria Rilke

✝

Dear Father,

"Look for the light in all things and in all people," says Rule for a New Brother. [14] But the life of a public minister presents many challenges that can be either obstacles to growth or opportunities for conversion. Take the opportunity, but recognize the danger in the uphill climb. It begins with a bit more cynicism and a little less openness. You are both serious and sensitive. It's tough to always look for the light when it's dark out. That is when we pray for the many gifts of the Holy Spirit, *one at a time.* We pray harden not our hearts O God with extra fervor. (Psalm 95: 8) But most of all, we remember his promise to be with us always.

You are never alone.

> In his great compassion he touches your heart now in its deepest recesses in what would otherwise be held a sanctuary apart protected there to remain hidden even from love himself.

(cf. Ezekiel 48:8)

Dear Father,

He loves you! May this simply be a reminder on days such as these when painful vulnerability brings about doubt, fear, anger, loneliness, and confusion.

Lucy glibly remarks, "We learn more from losing than winning," to which we might reply: 'Then I must be the smartest person in the whole world."[15] This is her interpretation of Matthew, no doubt. Bless the cloud that brings the fullness of his presence. (cf. Matthew 17:5)

The stars have "sharp corners and rough edges," says C.S. Lewis. But then, "Dream furniture is the only kind on which we never bang our toes or scrape our knees."[16]

Hold on to the vision you hold in your heart as you bow before him, this gentle, loving God, and know that you are his. Because of this, you can say to us do not be afraid and be heard. For this, we thank you. Perhaps we can assure you of the same. I sincerely hope so.

> Find the truth of oneself in the core of
> one's being which is beyond the reach of
> others, beyond the whims and invulner-
> able to the vagaries, where the standards
> for performance are not set by someone
> else and fidelity is defined from within.[17]
>
> —Anthony Padovano

Dear Father,

Jesus walked a very rocky road after he stopped to ask, is this what you want from me? In stillness, he received his answer. "This is my beloved son, with whom I am well pleased … listen to him" (Matthew 3:17).

In a moment, the face of God shone on the face of one so totally free, so utterly poor (cf 2 Corinthians 8:9).Gratefully, the process by which we are transfigured is slow and gradual.

In a moment of glory he received the strength to go on. Our moments of glory come in moments of intimacy where we are filled with awe, and he teaches us compassion and love. If in moments of doubt we step back and listen, he teaches us wisdom and gives us insight. A rich balance between the two is one of his many blessings.

Your ministry is a reflection of just such a relationship. May your moments of glory be many as you travel from strength to strength doing his will. Thank you for your dedication to prayer and your commitment to grow.

> Benedict says, "Interior freedom is to be earned after many years of work and patience. It is the last luxury to be won because personal interiority is the last mystery to be faced." [18]

✝

Dear Father,

Our community is becoming a living gift to others. Though you have been made to go where you would not have chosen to go, God has given you the interior freedom you need and he will bring your love to perfection.

Whether your prayer is an experience of infinite distance, or of the fullness of his being flowing into yours, allow yourself to be carried by the rhythm.[19] God has been incredibly gracious to you, my friend. May he continue to give you the grace to seek his will.

"When we stand in the middle of a transition, when we can no longer even remain standing; the changes which have taken place in our hearts easily feel as though nothing has or is happening, when in fact there are many signs which indicate that transformation is part of us long before it actually happens."[20]

—Rainer Maria Rilke

✝

Dear Father,

Those who come to celebrate with you wish to know how to pray, that they may live and love as you do. They stand in quiet awe of your strength to be alone when you so obviously need the closeness of others—your strength to surrender and painfully let go. They sense an extraordinary fidelity and experience priesthood marked by integrity upon which all else rests.[21]

They will, at the very least, question what has gone on between you and your God, perhaps discovering that the word dwells among us in service to others.

So in moments when you wonder why, remember those he has entrusted to your care recognize where your strength comes from and who it is that affects your life. Remember, Christ is alive, as we are faithful to ourselves, to him in us, and to those whom we serve in his name, then go rest!

"That I may preach without preaching, not by words but by example, by the catching force, the sympathetic influence of what I do, the evident fullness of the love my heart bears for you."[22]

—Mother Teresa

For the gift of conviction to live the gospel you have preached to us, Lord give us your conviction.

✝

Dear Father,

Each year we prepare with Holy Mother church for his coming...and "on this day we both mourn and rejoice at once and for the same reason," said the Archbishop of Canterbury. Each Advent we realize that he comes again and again to the place where we are; not through our decided effort, but in love, he comes. Lord Jesus Christ, son of the living God, "...what works will be done between Christmas and Easter?" [23] "How will you respond to the ordinary moments in your life?" you ask. In prayerful reflection you challenge us, in gratitude we recognize this merciful and loving *God* is *with us.*

> There once was a monk who came down from his cave once a year to play with the children. He said, "Last year I was a miserable monk. This year, nothing has changed." [24]

✝

Dear Father,

If you have arrived at the Easter vigil having had the best of intentions to celebrate fully his rising in a more profound way than ever before, you are not alone.

Easter comes upon us nonetheless. In our trials and hopes, he steers our minds and hearts as we are asked to study the scriptures more carefully, give more generously, follow the Lord more tenaciously, and allow the spirit to reach the deepest part of our being. He asks us to respond with our very best self from the place where we are.

The church has provided reverent liturgies, silence, the office, and opportunity for renewal and reconciliation. A thread deliberately binds the weeks together in prayerful invitation; come closer, sink deeper. Dare to step beyond this place to find the incarnate God at the tomb where he makes himself known anew, again and again and again.

A Zen master was invited to a monastery to give instructions in Zen practice. He exhorted the monks to solve their koan but an old monk maintained "Our way is different." We have been praying without effort, waiting to be illumined by the grace of God. The Zen master laughed and said, "We believe that God has already done his share.[25]"

Dear Father,

It's hard to believe that you are celebrating another anniversary. To renew your commitment this year is unlike any other. It seems the contextual framework once needed is dying as he ever so gently supplants it with himself. With time the perfectionist is embraced by tolerance. The priest travels from image to likeness. Priesthood becomes less burdensome and relationships grow. The thinker sees the world more often through his heart now as he celebrates the internal liturgy more freely. This has truly been a year of grace.

This has truly been a year of deep abiding love, of changes and blessings for which we share your gratitude.

> "I've been a monk for twenty-five years and haven't gotten a thing out of it."[26]

Dear Father,

I pray that your feast day be a reminder of that moment of glory. I pray that its ageless wisdom allows you to be still, watch, and listen. May that same voice strengthen and guide you on the path to Jerusalem.

The Transfiguration "does not exist for its own sake," says Susanna Wesley. "It exists to clothe the common things with a radiance they never had before."[27] Our common life seems to be filled with that reality, though we are not typically afforded the luxury of such an astonishing perspective. Meditating on the events as they happened, gaining insight into the tie between the old and the new was another time and another place. How much more difficult it is for us now to capture, in a moment, the view from afar while totally committed to the very presence of that moment.

Jesus went to pray and seek the will of God. A moment to be still and listen assured him. He continued on the road to Jerusalem. May this celebration renew your conviction to do the same.

> "The memory is carved like an inscription on the rocks along my way. O Israel, yes, I remember, and the memory reminds me to have confidence." [28]

Befriending

If we are faithful to the journey, we will inevitably collide with our humanity. Discovery of the divine requires the vulnerability of disclosure. To befriend another in the spiritual life is to navigate the unknown. The celibate faces a challenge which is unlike any other for which there are few instructions.

Dear Father,

Peck defined love as "the will to extend one-self for the purpose of nurturing one's own or another's spiritual growth."[29] John Donne, in *Reasons of the Heart,* might change will to will-ingness, for he sees the willingness to be loved and known as central to our ever being able to truly love and be known by another or God. [30]

But sacred space is created in darkness and invites one to meet another at a place where we are most alone, most afraid, most ourselves. As in the Sign of Jonas, Merton "rides to the deeper monster places where God, self, other, and the world are impenetrable."[31]

No greater gift can be given another than the depth of this unspeakable place; a gift that can never be forgotten.

> As Lincoln, Shakespeare, and Jesus—friends not only in time and space—but friends of all the human race. They made

the universe their own, and yet from that high seat can stoop and speak with each of us alone. [32]

"... to pass through the mirror of their own reflection to see from the perspective of others in order to imagine what it's like in the other's world then return home with their world enlarged, enriched, deepened without suffering through the distorted, frightening, lonely, journey of fantasy." [33]

—Through the Looking Glass

Dear Father,

Is love the love of Shel Silverstein's *Giving Tree,* which allows all things without question or reservation?[34] Is it that of *Lafcadio, the Lion Who Shot Back*, which boasts I AM, listen to me! [35]

In exploring the love of the giving tree, the vision of such transcendence fascinates me, as does learning to say "I am" gracefully. What begins in the spirit will continue by his grace, understanding that humility is endless…

> "The highest does not stand without the lowest."[36]

> "simul justus et peccator"

> "Humans are akin to angels and tom-cats, that's why Francis called the body 'brother ass,' because everyone should be able to take a divine joke."[37]
>
> —C.S. Lewis

Dear Father,

Fully human comes before fully divine. The homily was on celibacy this weekend. The celebrant said this about his own life: "I'm a person first with feelings and needs, then a Christian, and finally a priest." He said, "The more humanized I become, the more divinized I can be," then went on to talk about the humanity of Jesus Christ.

Father, you are an excellent priest! May God give you peace and guide you in his path. Rejoice with the church that he has called us friends. His mercy and love endures forever.

> We come to see the experience of love in our own lives as mirrors in which we can contemplate the divine love.
>
> —Chang Tzu[38]

✝

Dear Father,

Rejoice, my friends, in the love that you share; for in love a very real part of who we are is accepted, understood, and affirmed, says Donne.

> We are right to thank God who has given such power to men. Let us make no mistake; love which calls us up and out of ourselves is not so very different from the contemplative love which we seek. Neither relationship will be forced. The transformation to a greater love will not be an act of the will. Dr. Tyrell says that the best advice we can give those on their way to contemplative love who find themselves overtaken by human love is to slow down and experience love.

We are alone together, he goes on to say, and we cannot make each other un-alone.[39]

"The heart has its reasons that reason knows nothing of …"

—Pascal

First touched by heart's reason and then by mind's reason one is apprehended by reality before one comprehends that reality. [40]

—Plato

☩

Dear Father,

Life is harsh, it is limited and imperfect.[41] In accepting life's harshness, we lose the obsession with perfection. We learn to live in loving acceptance with others who are equally imperfect. With acceptance comes a deeper loneliness, yet a more genuine intimacy with self, others, and God. We recognize feelings are good and normal, thus can we move "from relatedness to relationship."[42]

> "Empty yourself so that you may be filled; go out so that you can go in," says Augustine.

> " ... let each one of you be together, but alone, even as the strings of a lute are alone though they quiver with the same music."[43]

Dear Father,

Denial of feelings inhibits human nature, it's true. St. Thomas Aquinas would say such impediment is a tinkering with the work of grace. An experience of human love has the potential of promoting a poverty that St. John of the Cross believes is fertile ground for the Holy Spirit. Love, though, will most certainly leave us vulnerable. There is no safety in love. God does not ensure against heartbreak. "The hues of divine love became those of human tears to show he understands. Truly, the mystical body of Christ takes radiance in our love for another." [44]

> The student asks the master if he wishes
> for him to pray that his trials be removed.
> The master answers, pray, rather, that I
> be faithful through them.

Penitence

Suffering

There is no rising without dying and pain is inevitable in the process of becoming 'known'. There can be no transformation without walking the road he first travelled for us.

Dear Father,

It seems this past year has been filled with endless struggles. It has been fraught with a series of hurts insisting, if not demanding, your attention. You have not allowed yourself defense or escape (as so many of us would) to preserve precious space. Exposed and vulnerable, you have nonetheless faced difficult times with a great deal of courage. Sure, it's not over yet. There is much work to do, but then there always will be. Right now, you need time to re-create the spirit. One of the problems with your vocation, though, is this stage you seem to live on. Many will not understand or accept you not being totally available. So be sure that the place from which you decide to slow down is a place that says with certainty, *It is okay for me to be here right now.*

Father, whether you are passing around warm hugs or putting us at arm's length because you feel overwhelmed, know that it's okay, and you are loved as you are. Whether you are preaching a powerful homily, celebrating a beautiful liturgy, or not finding the time to visit the sick or intervene in one more family crisis, know that you are an excellent priest. What you cannot do does not detract from or change what you do. Whether you have been touched by his intimate presence today in contemplation or haven't prayed at all, know that you are holy in his sight always, and be at peace.

> "My life has been spent lowering my expectations."[45]

> "non confundas me ab expectatione mea"[46]

> Do not let me be frustrated by my expectations (Psalm 119: 118)

Dear Father,

Our Lord used many pulpits during his
life, but when he mounted his pulpit for
the last time, the cross, like all orators he
looked over his audience. Far off in Jerusalem he could see the gilded roof of the
temple reflecting its rays against the sun,
which was soon to hide its face in shame.
There beyond the temple walls he could
catch a glimpse of those who were strain-
ing their eyes to see him whom the darkness knew not. At the edge of the crowd
were timid followers ready to flee in case
of danger. There also were the execution-
ers getting their dice ready to shake for
his garments. Close to the cross was the
only apostle present, John, whose face was
like a cast molded out of love. Magdalene
was there and, of course, his mother.

> Mary, Magdalene and John—inno-
> cence, penitence, and priesthood; the
> three types of souls forever to be found
> beneath the cross of Christ. [47]

What is your view from the pulpit, my friend, of those whom you serve? You too must see the vision from afar while just before you sit a people of mixed loyalties at best. What is his view as you sit close to his cross as one chosen and alone suffering to imitate such love? These have truly been difficult days for you. The pain of rejection, the loneliness is apparent. Evident as well is your struggle to grow in holiness while attempting to serve a stubborn people.

I hear Job say, "…I am exhausted and my spirit is broken." I hear, "Do not lose heart my son, for God will not abandon you. He will not forget your work and the love you have shown him by your service past and present." (Job 16:7–17:1)

Hope extends beyond the veil through which Jesus has entered in your behalf being made high priest forever (cf. Hebrews: 6:19–20).

May Jesus our Lord furnish you with all that is good, with all that you need. In the love reflected from beneath the cross, may we come to see in our fragile humanity that powerful divinity which is our comfort our joy and our strength.

> "Let nothing trouble thee, let nothing affright thee, all things are passing, God never changes, patience obtains everything, nothing is wanting to him who possesses God. God alone suffices."

> St. Theresa's bookmark [48]

Dear Bishop,

I am deeply concerned about the young priests struggling in the first days and years of service to the Lord. The heart at the center of holy mother church lies in the priesthood, says our beloved Holy Father.[49] Yet many, so very many, struggle with discouragement, disappointment, even disbelief in the current state of affairs. How can this be God's loving hand at work in joyful creation? Christian joy shines from a life of deep faith in peace and utter silence. They know this. But a cynical hatch, match, and dispatch as quickly as possible to get to choir practice and the bulletin before the women's club meets is not far away. All in the life of a parish priest, you say? What about prayer? What about the need for community? What about simply wasting time with God? Between which two appointments is the relationship nurtured? Is it just a matter of organization? Who do you say no to? Which person or persons does one choose? Who else will do it?

How do you justify *I need* when the world hungers for the truth?

There has been much upon which to reflect these days—too much at one time. Perhaps this is a time less to think than to listen.

> Once the brothers said to Pambo, "Speak to the Bishop that he might be edified." Pambo said, "If he is not edified by my silence, my speech will certainly not edify him."[50]

✝

Dear Father,

The circle of those we trust is drawn tighter when we feel used and abused, bought with dreams and sold for lack of worldly ambition; when the larger church seems to have delivered us into the hands of our enemies. If Christ is free to wear a crown of thorns one day and eat breakfast on the beach with his friends a short while later, certainly he has freed us to do the same.[51]

Free, yes, but it is difficult to be standing in a clearing. You fought to be recognized as a servant worthy of trust. You sought to share your ministry with your brothers. It is difficult because it goes beyond these things, doesn't it?

"It is faith that gives us the freedom to suffer the exposure of our uniqueness and the vulnerability of our dreams one day and grow in the grace of life's humor the next."[52]

Jesus let go of his life and entered into a profound union with the father from which Easter occurred.[53] As we let go and believe, we enter into communion with one another and find that Christ is alive and Easter just happened ... then move on.

"Joy is deeper yet than agony."

—Friedrich Nietzsche

Dear Father,

There is an ancient Buddhist tradition in which monks collect alms, food, or money from lay supporters with a begging bowl sometimes given to them with their robes at ordination. It not only has historical significance associated with Buddha, but has become a symbol of his teachings on non-attachment. Each morning the monks from the surrounding monasteries go into the villages and towns where they wait in silence for the people to place their "gift" into the bowl.

The Japanese translation of begging bowl is "just enough" or "Oryoki."

Whenever I feel overwhelmed, I recall two things: the serenity prayer and the begging bowl.

c Elizabeth Vigeon

This is the only moment there is;
the only moment in which we can enter now.
Now is just enough.

> "God, grant me the serenity to accept the
> things I cannot change, the courage to
> change the things I can, and the wisdom
> to know the difference."[54]

✝

Dear Father,

Charlie Brown frantically runs around trying to organize his baseball players into a close-knit team. While repeatedly devastated, he continues to believe in the basic goodness of man.[55]

Priesthood, too, is a sign of such hope. Hope gives us the courage to risk, knowing life is only meaningful if we reach out to others. Hope allows us to face the uncertainty of truth and love when quite often we would prefer life to be as predictable as a math problem. In love, we confront an immeasurable mystery and are called to bear witness and exclaim with St. Paul:

> Yet my brothers I do not consider myself to have arrived spiritually nor do I consider myself perfect but I keep going on grasping ever more firmly the purpose for which Jesus Christ grasped me. My brothers, I do not consider myself to have grasped it even now. I go straight for the

goal, my reward the honor of my high
calling by God in Jesus Christ
(cf. Phillipians 3: 12–14).

"To be earnest in seeking the truth is an
indispensible requisite for finding it."[56]
—John Henry Newman

✝

Dear Father,

I lift you up before him who loves you. I pray that you might know the warmth of his embrace when you feel most alone, know the strength of his mighty arm when you are weary, and his comfort when you're afraid. When one possesses a sincerity of heart and an openness of spirit, there will inevitably be moments of great pain along the way.

We can trust him implicitly when all too often the only thing we know is that which we do not know.[57] He truly is the Alpha and the Omega and nothing exists outside of him!

So I pray that you experience his love in both the whole of creation and this moment, in which you simply are his. I pray that he give you the grace you need to continue this journey with love.

> "…believe in a love that is being stored up for you like an inheritance, and have faith that in this love there is a strength

and a blessing so large that you can travel
as far as you wish without having to step
outside it." [58]

—Rainer Maria Rilke

Dear Father,

Encouraged and humbled; emerge from the many trials in which he continues to mold you like fire-tried gold. We are brought to our knees by the ever-present love and grace of God, realized more intuitively than emotionally in our innermost struggles. He is so awesome, so mysterious! I am rambling in gratitude.

May God fill you with his blessings as you bathe in his light. May he strengthen you in his love, community, and friendships. May he guide you toward an even greater love and understanding of his presence in your life and grant you peace.

Reconciling

"To you, Oh God, every heart stands open, and every will speaks, no secret is hidden from you."[59]

Reconciliation is the grace by which we are sanctified. It is the process by which the 'window' of the soul is made clean. With the Eucharist, through prayer, sacrifice, courage and perseverance, hearts are purified so his glory may be proclaimed before all the nations.

Dear Father,

Thankfully, "God does not ask did you succeed or fail," says Au in *By Way of the Heart,* but rather "did your imperfections teach you to trust my love and better understand the mystery of inequity in the lives of others?"[60]
Similarly, Thich Nhat Hanh admits:

> I am the 12-year-old girl, refugee on a small boat, who throws herself into the ocean after being raped by a sea pirate, and I am the pirate, my heart not yet capable of seeing and loving.[61]

His everlasting mercy allows us to be incomplete yet complete, estranged yet related, distorted yet fulfilled. It feels very distorted some days, doesn't it? It's the messiness of life. I recall countless references to humanity and divinity and the crucible of his love. With frayed edges, we smile and cry at once while thanking God.

Brother, please remember, rather, the intention of the heart, which incessantly begs for purification, rather than any accidental success in following his will. While the heart remains both estranged and related, I know the promise of forgiveness and his indisputable faithfulness will prevail.

> "I do not see the road ahead, I cannot know where it will lead for certain nor do I know myself and the fact that I think I am following your will does not mean that I am actually doing so but I believe that the desire to please you does in fact please you and I hope I have that desire in all that I do. I hope I will never do anything apart from that desire and I know you will lead me through the right road though I may seem to be lost." [62]

—Thomas Merton

> "Men proceed from light to light, always struggling, always reaffirming, always resuming their march. Often halting, loitering, straying, delaying, returning, yet following, no other way."[63]

—T.S. Eliot

✝

Dear Father,

I once heard a story of two bumper stickers. One read "I've found it," the other, "I've lost it, keep on doubting." The first wishes to announce newfound life in Christ. The second wants to make it absolutely clear that no matter how deep our faith, no one on this side of the grave has ever quite found it. God holds us in-between.

> Doubt is the good by which we are driven to transcend ourselves. Faith in Christ does not obliterate doubt. In the true pilgrim faith and doubt coexist. The latter drives him on the journey, the former gives him grounds for hope. To come to a doubt, preached John Donne, to a debate in any religious duty is the voice of God in our conscience. If you wish to know the truth, doubt and then you will inquire.[64]

What if we learned to just live the question?

Dear Father,

Some days it seems the Snoopys of the world abound; waltzing off oblivious to the fact that they have just somehow tied you up in knots.[65]

What makes the bad days bad and the good days good? What is right before our very eyes on the bad days that are the very thing from which he wishes most to free us? What, on the good days, is his gentle way of loving us where we need it most? Both are because he loves us so much. It makes things simpler somehow, doesn't it? [66]

> How do you know, if you are on the right path? When things are going well? When things are not going well?
> —Friends of the Holy Spirit

Dear Father,

Thomas Merton says contradictions will always exist in the souls of men. We are not meant to resolve them but to live with them and see them in the light of exterior and objective values that make them trivial by comparison.[67]

> Max Picard says, "sanctity is being in a silence, which so reconciles the contradictions within us, that although they remain there they cease to be a problem. It is necessary to name him in whose silence he alone knows my name. In silence he calls me my son and I am aware of him as my father. In silence, I know that I am and I cry Abba, Father. My own voice is only able to rouse a dead echo when it calls out. There will never be any awakening in me unless I am called out of darkness by my God." [68]

Silence is our salvation. I believe this with all my being.

> "An empty sort of mind is valuable for finding pearls and tails and things, because it can see what's in front of it. An overstuffed mind is unable to. While the clear mind listens to the birds singing, the stuffed full of knowledge and cleverness mind wonders what kind of bird is singing."[69]
>
> —Winnie the Pooh

Dear Father,

What a relief, a stroke of remorse. If the prodigal son knew his father would not censure him, would he have returned home? Penance makes the sacrament of reconciliation possible. Otherwise, how could anyone bear to be loved that much? Please take back your robe; I wish only to be your slave. I am an unmerciful sinner. I know, he says, and gives you his ring and sandals instead (cf Luke 15:11–32).

Can we expect more (or less) than this from ourselves? More love than we can tolerate, more love than we can give? "He has come home, because he believed in someone larger than his guilt, in a love more faithful than his own love, in a heart that never disregards the sacrifice others make to be where they are, in arms that offer mercy, in hands that bless and heal." [70]

> "And even if … you have done all things well you will still be an unprofitable servant."[71]

Dear Father,

If I could just touch his clothing, longed the woman with the hemorrhage. What was her experience of suffering that led to this moment of truth? There was nothing left to give but her very self over to the only one who could help her. All else had failed, all else had been taken away. There was nothing else and no one left to turn to.

Even thoughts of death lose their sting and attraction. If I just touch his clothing ... with no energy left to plead her cause, too exhausted to even resist his unconditional love.

"The mind creates the abyss," says Nisargadatta, "and then the heart crosses it." [72]

"Father," cries the heart in its vertiginous plunge, "into your hands which I do not feel, which open to let me fall, which will catch me at the bottom of this abyss, into your hands I entrust my spirit, into your hands I breathe out my spirit, my holy spirit!"[73]

We are Broken

"As I write you now about our broken-
ness, I recall a scene from Leonard Bern-
stein's mass, written for John F. Kennedy
that embodied for me the thought of bro-
kenness put under the blessing. Toward
the end of this work, the priest, richly
dressed in splendid liturgical vestments,
is lifted up by his people. He towers high
above the adoring crowd carrying in
his hands a glass chalice. Suddenly, the
human pyramid collapses and the priest
comes tumbling down. His vestments are
ripped off, and his glass chalice falls to
the ground and is shattered. As he walks
through the debris of his former glory—
barefoot, wearing only blue jeans and a
tee shirt—children's voices are heard
singing, 'Laude, Laude, Laude.' Suddenly
the priest notices the broken chalice. He

looks at it for a long time and then, halt-ingly, he says, 'I never realized that bro-ken glass could shine so brightly.'"[74]

Life of the Beloved

—Henri Nouwen

Priesthood

Awakening

Through his atonement, he takes each being to himself and without destroying its reality confers upon it a new being. But you still think it is a dream. Rub the sleep from your eyes. You are free to go wherever you please.[75]

✝

Dear Father,

You began your ministry with an act of surrender and affirmation of faith. God beckoned you by name to a deeper union. In touching humanity, you touch divinity, and discover:

> "Only in love can you reveal to me your richness my God. Only through grace may I recognize the eternal word of the Father's heart. Only in love may you become the triune God of my life. Because only in love can I find you, my God. Only in love can I find my way home."[76]
>
> —Karl Rahner

Ah-ha moments! They are precious and few. They are strung together and adorn the tree of life until that final moment when the eyes of our eyes see and the purpose for which we were created is revealed. One inexplicable moment ... and life is changed forever.

Dear Father,

There is a story told by an old monk about a family who saved their whole lives for enough money to take a boat to another land. Some only had enough for the fare, so their friends all bought them something to eat when they left, except everyone brought bread and cheese! After a couple of weeks of eating only bread and cheese, one of the children told his father "I simply can't eat bread and cheese one more day!"

Duly chastised for his lack of gratitude, the boy went without eating as he had promised until, unable to bear the hunger, he left their meager surroundings in search of food on the upper decks of the ship. There he saw a most magnificent sight—a table larger than their home overflowing with foods of all kinds. "Please, sir," he asked, "may I have a small bit of fish?" "But, of course," the large man replied, "The food is included in the fare."[77]

"You can become preoccupied with the acquiring of virtue and miss the whole point."[78]

Dear Father,

"A century ago, a young student at the great Oxford University in England was taking an important examination in religious studies. The examination question for this day was to write about the religious and spiritual meaning in the miracle of Christ turning water into wine."

(In just hearing the question I immediately thought of a dozen different approaches and wanted a blue book and pencil so I could answer it myself. Those are the questions you dream of in theology. The students in that class were not unlike me, except for the young student.)

"For two hours he sat in the crowded classroom while other students filled their pages with long essays to show their understanding. The exam time was almost over, and this one student had not written a single word. The proctor came over to him and insisted that he commit something to paper before turning it in. The young Lord Byron simply picked up his hand and penned the following line: "The water met its master, and blushed."[79]

> "God is the 'boundaryless, wordless,
> whoosh of suchness.'" [80]

—Stephen Levine

Namaste

✝

Years of study and prayer is reflected in every homily given, service prepared, teaching enjoined. Every servant's heart has been melted and molded to proclaim Christ risen yesterday, today and always. Every committed soul is on a journey in time—not a beginning, middle or an end—just *now*. So until that moment when we are again in his arms, we continue this journey of faith ...

The following is a glimpse into one life of prayer begging supplication for its Church and their anointed ones.

Journey of Faith is the story of one communicant from the pew. That is all. It is my story. What is yours?

Part II—A Journey of Faith in Prayer and Meditation

A *Journey of Faith* includes an assortment of essays, a collection of journal entries, and prayers. An essay or memoir begins each chapter providing the background relevant to that particular part of the journey. The collection of writings that follow each story occurred over a span of forty plus years. They are organized as a linear course which is not to suggest that the spiritual life obeys some artificial timetable. It is neither tidy nor predictable because God eludes all boundaries—always has and always will.

Spiritual seekers around the world each have a story. It is those stories that accumulate and give basis to the evolution of a call and a choice. This is where *A Journey of Faith in Prayer and Meditation* begins; with a story followed by choosing a path which becomes a longing, demanding renunciation before sight is restored and revelation becomes possible.

"The glory of God is man fully alive," said Iraneus.[81] What does it mean to be "fully alive" and how does it manifest God's glory? These questions marked the beginning of a deliberate journey more than thirty years ago. Since then, my longing to proclaim my own profound fiat has led to a progressive renunciation, a "via negativa" as it were.[82] This journey in search of at-one-ment or no-self has indeed been one of endless humility. Unlike anything I could ever expect or imagine, the nature of his glory continues to unfold.

"Make use of a method when you need it … and as you pray … you will discover the wide horizon of each prayer," says *Rule for a New Brother*.[83] Ambrose, fourth century bishop of Milan, said, "All that is true, by whomever it has been said, is from the Holy Spirit."

While I have always been and continue to be a practicing Catholic, my search for God has included an amazing adventure in other methods. My introduction to Eastern spirituality began on a monastic retreat along with an appreciation for silence inherent in both meditation and contemplative prayer. In the context of contemplative prayer and insight meditation, or Vipassana, union with the living God and no-self are not so different after all. There appears to be more congruence between contemplative spirituality and Buddhist psychology than otherwise apparent. One naturally fosters the growth and practice of the other. "But Christianity is a highly personalized religion, and Buddhism advocates self-annihilation: where is the common ground?" asks countless inquirers of the East-West traditions.

It is in the depths of one's own heart, says Don Juan that such things are learned, and it is out of the depths of my own heart that I now share my experience of the common ground in search of glory.[84]

Beginning

c Elizabeth Vigeon

Firsts—Live or Die

What is it about firsts that hits me square in the chest with pangs of fear? Is it the unknown? Is it the imagination? Is it the sense of powerlessness or the fear of failure? What stops me dead in my tracks at the threshold of nearly every beginning I can recall?

Dead is an interesting word to use in the context of first, but fear, like a vector of impending doom, seems to threaten the life of all that is familiar, concrete, in control, and successful. I didn't know this standing at the threshold of first grade. I hadn't even grasped it by twenty-six on my first visit to the Buddhist monastery; two firsts that had a lot more in common than readily apparent.

Windmill Street School was a massive showcase of adjoining brick buildings. It extended beyond an entire corner block. Its incline required the immense concrete staircase to rise to an unimaginable three levels. A sweeping cement banister bordered this one hundred-year-old masterpiece. Its height generously exceeding my own was wide enough to accommodate the bottom of a moderately sized child. Iced with pink and beige marble, it looked more like a waterslide than a balustrade.

At six, I stood at the base of this stone monster gazing in awe at the three distinct landings exposing angled entries. The metal doors, newly painted, reflected strategically placed teachers nearly transfigured by the early morning light. There was nothing at all familiar about this vantage. It may well have been at a new school in a different town because, as kindergartners, the street lined entrance was off-limits.

How would I negotiate the immense risers? What if I tripped? Undoubtedly, those slippery chunks on either side did not offer any reassurance whatsoever. After all, it was not so long ago that I traded metal braces for leather-laced boots. They were equally ugly but less noticeable to support my clumsy legs. Even if I did reach the safety of a landing, where and to whom would I go? Faced with foreign ground, envisioning the worst possible outcome, I stood frozen until shaken by the sudden blast of the bell threatening my balance, even before I started.

The Insight Meditation Society (IMS) appeared over the hill. The narrow, winding road led to an old Benedictine monastery nestled in the forest. The sprawling brick building with its majestic, white columns had become the retreat center for Buddhist teachings. Metta, or loving-kindness, replaced Pax above the doorway. A lone stained-glass window remained to protect the basement on the far left of the building. It depicted the proverbial Christ in the garden, which offered little consolation.

At twenty-six, I drove slowly toward the graveled driveway, sharply aware of each stone disturbed by the weight of the tires. The first uncertainty struck. Where do I park? This nearly paralyzed me. I prayed some fledgling like me would inquire so I could unwittingly follow suit, but there was no such miracle. A flat dirt area beyond the building with traces of trampled grass lay adjacent to the circular drive. It was then that

I noticed a wooden brace with a placard attached: NO PARKING IN THE DRIVEWAY. Did that mean no stopping in the driveway? I would look foolish dragging all my stuff up this hill. Plagued by this dilemma, I decided being wrong was better than looking foolish; I had my fill of the latter. But foolish was not nearly finished with me yet. Armed with pillows, blankets, sleeping bag, a very large suitcase, and a stash of food and caffeine, I felt duly protected by familiarity and control. I didn't even notice that *stuff* for the veteran meditators consisted of a sole parcel like a backpack slung over one shoulder. I proceeded to the appointed lot and dragged my stymied self up the hill. Several people were meandering as I made my way up the few cement steps that formed an apron around the oversized front door.

The vestibule was neatly lined with an array of footwear. I glanced about quickly, seeking direction, but found none. To my right, closed French doors revealed a room with wall-to-wall bookcases. A large, red embroidered cloth hung above the fireplace. An eclectic group of old overstuffed chairs circled the room. Taped to one of the small glass panes the sign read:

NO READING, EATING, or
NAPPING IN THE LIBRARY

How odd. "Does anyone know where you register for the retreat?" My booming voice cracked the pervasive silence and nearly derailed me. A tall, thin, bald figure in saffron robes—his dark, deep eyes avoiding my inquisitive gaze—gestured toward a framed entry into a large dining room. The odor of curried something assaulted my nostrils. I was grateful for the smuggled sustenance tucked in my suitcase. I made my way over to one of many long tables upon which several neatly stacked papers and a small metal box represented the only sign of activity. Silence prevailed. The young woman seated at the table handed me a half sheet of paper that read:

> I will not hold IMS liable should any misfortune occur while I am here.
>
> Signed _____

A gasp stuck in my throat like a large piece of ice. The pen in my trembling fingers betrayed the dread that exploded my imagination. It was clear. This was unfamiliar territory, and I was not in control. My first instinct was to flee, but my discalced feet remained fixed to the chilly vinyl floor.

The blast of the morning bell must have mobilized my rigid body to the appropriate landing, because soon I was considering the danger in the slope back down with slightly more courage.

The gentle sound of the Tibetan bell resounded at perfect intervals. At the front of the meditation hall, the tall, thin man in orange appeared regal as he took his place on the cushion and read:

> *The Guest House*
> This being human is a guest house
> Every morning a new arrival.
> A joy, a depression, a meanness,
> Some momentary awareness comes
> As an unexpected visitor.
> Welcome and entertain them all!
> Even if they're a crowd of sorrows

Who violently sweep your house
Empty of its furniture.
Still treat each guest honorably.
He may be clearing you out
For some new delight.
The dark thought, the shame, the malice,
Meet them at the door laughing,
And invite them in (for tea.)
Be grateful for whoever comes,
because each has been sent
as a guide from beyond.[85]

I listened from the comfort of my zafu and realized that I had stayed for tea, grateful I didn't die.

Thus my journey began. Sunanda, a young Christian woman from France, was the meditation teacher that weekend. This gentle woman, an act of surrender, and a "beginner's mind" taught me to meditate.[86]

I learned to watch as an imperceptible shadow standing just slightly behind the pain without being the pain, slightly behind the rage without becoming the rage, yet completely aware of it and nothing else. Learning to observe from slightly behind the thoughts, watching them come, letting them go, without dragging the nets, without changing a thing, without thrusting aside. Allowing it all to rise, have its presence acknowledged, without so much as a disturbance in the rhythm of the breath, before letting it go. Always, at every moment, at every hour, returning the attention to the place at the gate of the temple to simply watch, undisturbed. Just watch.

> Chiang Tzu said, "The perfect man uses his mind as a mirror. It grasps nothing, it refuses nothing, it receives, but does not keep." [87]

If we meditate on the breath in and out, the rhythm of the universe is realized in the simple acceptance of gift and the task of letting go.

> "If you do not come too close" you will recognize the palm of his hand.[88]

Prayer is too closely linked with the things that go on inside us and through the events of everyday life, remarks Hume. When we cannot focus on God, because "God cannot be known by thought; prayer becomes distasteful."[89] Thus, we are forced into just being and silence exposes the illusions we've held so dear.[90]

Dear Lord,

Beginning again, dancing about in the 'on-deck circle', it is with gratitude and love in "a heart held humble to level and light the way" that I return.[92] All points lead to the greater glory of God. Thank you.

Lost

Standstill (instructed the Elder to chil-
  dren who may become lost in the forest.)
The trees ahead and the bushes
  beside you are not lost.
Wherever you are is called here.
And you must treat it as a
  powerful stranger,
Must ask permission to know
  it and to be known.
The forest breathes. Listen. It answers.
I have made this place around you.
If you leave it, you may come
  back again, saying Here.
No two trees are the same to Raven.
No two branches are the same to Wren.
If what a tree or bush does is lost on you
You are surely lost. Stand-
  still. The forest knows
Where you are, you must let it find you.[91]

Choosing

The Call

Samuel cried, "Here I am, Lord" (1Samuel 3:4). Abraham abandoned his homeland to sojourn in the wilderness (Genesis 21:34). Moses fled into the desert, and we remain in awe. These biblical giants listened, heard, and responded (Exodus 2:15). The call of God-with-us prevails (Matthew 1:23).

The morning chill lingered. The bells resounded with an invitation to worship. They held no warning that a summons would supplant the habitual jaunt toward the vestibule with a piercing dread. As if struck by a bolt of lightning, I remained motionless upon the landing. *Am I being called to religious life?* The question so dominated the moment that it rendered all else impenetrable. Aware only of a fierce rebuttal forming in my pounding heart, I hadn't noticed the moist chill wrapped in wrenched palms lying stiffly at my side. Preposterous! I must have appeared visibly shaken but pretended to be simply preoccupied.

I was grateful for the lapse, which created some urgency to begin liturgy. Comforted by the rhetoric, I successfully dismissed the proposal, but not the encounter.

Our lives are filled with endless crossroads. The choices we make both large and small have far-reaching effects, many of which we never truly grasp. "When the young man asked, 'what must I do to possess eternal life?' he went away sad because he couldn't make the total commitment, not because he didn't want to."[93] It is rather our response "to the call and the question of God,"

said Bonhoeffer, "as opposed to the result of that call."[94]

The apostles responded by immediately abandoning their nets to follow him. The nets that we are asked to abandon are our work, our reluctance, our successes, and responsibilities. Not so immediately do we abandon these. We come more slowly. We so covet our time and talent. It is an extraordinary challenge to choose a spiritual life. In sophisticated and subtle ways, we often distance ourselves from God rather than deepen a relationship of intimacy. The closer we become to our own hearts and minds, the closer we come to God, then realize exactly what it is he is asking of us. He asks nothing less than to die with him, nothing less than to go beyond our limits, while resting in his promise of mercy and love.

Holiness is a "condition of complete simplicity costing not less than everything," says Eliot.[95]

Silesius once said, "God is the circle's center for those who dare embrace him. For those who merely stand in awe, he is the circle's rim."

Do we choose to stand in awe rather than embrace—dare to embrace—the living God? Does our life of prayer help us create the circle's rim or become the circle's center?[96]

"Being one with the universe, with our darkest enemy, and with God; that is what we wish for most, whether we know it or not," says Kunkel.[97]

Spiritual life is often described as a journey, a discovery of what it means to be human; the discovery of a "love great enough to bear the risk of both disclosure and discovery," says Merton.[98]

"It has not been primarily my seeking and searching that has been most important," says Muilenberg, "rather the awareness of being sought and found by another."[99]

Being found by the living God is about intention and grace, call and response, and presence.

Blessed are those who hunger and thirst for holiness, they shall be filled. (cf Matthew 5:6)

"Systems move in seemingly random, disorderly ways until it chooses a new direction at a higher level of expanded consciousness." Are we but systems seeking a higher consciousness?[100] After living in random disorder, the systems theory is hopeful, though the heart is not always.

Fear though will often precede the knowing and knowing, once it occurs, is so much simpler than imagined, we barely notice without the drama.

Dear Lord,

May the grace of God and the assistance of his angels guide this journey. "Harden not my heart" (Psalm 95: 8), and help me to accept all things as part of a mystery greater than I could ever imagine. Help me to simply be still and listen. Amen.

Longing

Inside My Grandmother's Kitchen

The scent of lemon drifted in the air like fairy
dust, nearly taking on the color of the tender veins of the freshly cut fruit from which
the clear, spiced droplets were drizzled. A soft,
dusted pouch of kneaded dough waited patiently
on the table like a well-protected jewel trans-
parently encased. A thin, cotton cloth, its faded
blue stripes camouflaged by generous amounts of
flour, draped over the mound.

Perched at the threshold, my excitement
grew much larger than my tiny frame could
hold. I made my way across the cracked, check-
ered brown tone linoleum of my grandmother's
kitchen to the only empty seat at the table.

Criss cross, criss cross. The soft mound was gathered from its place of honor to be deftly divided. Twin puffs were swiftly rolled and snaked across the surface. Twisting to form a perfect braid, they turned to meet, forming an equally perfect circle.

The bustle in the air might appear to the non-familial eye as mildly chaotic. Everyone in the kitchen seemed to be speaking, though not necessarily to one another. I recognized the order of things immediately, just as I had each year at Easter as far back as I could remember.

I took my place, kneeling on the red vinyl chair. Like being lifted onto familiar shoulders at a parade, my exposed bony knees recognized the cracks and creases with a tuft of graying stuffing always threatening to poke through. The bulging chrome frame served as my protec-tion from the large, soft bodies donning breast-covered aprons darting about the room. It, too, proudly displayed years of clinking together to fit yet another stray piece of furniture (destined to become seating apparatus) for yet another boisterous voice at the door.

The sun-streaked room danced with anticipation as the creak from the oven door matched by a waving arm and the shout of "It's hot!" announced it's unnecessary warning. The sound of the old chipped porcelain door was sufficient for even the smallest member in the room to halt until the warm waft of freshly baked bread diminished.

I slipped off the chair as yet another creation was safely deposited on the crowded rack. I weaved clumsily through the billows of cotton prints and stood in the doorway of one of the two bedrooms flanking the encompassing view from the oven door. I gazed at the makeshift clotheslines strung about the room, towering over the pure white sheets donning the wall-to-wall beds and oversized bureau.

Countless strands of freshly made pasta lay carefully drying. My sisters and cousins darted among the cloaks, squealing with delight, and the chase was on. Suddenly a wisp of a floured mopine brushed my shoulder clearly in an effort to shoo the offenders from the sanctuary holding Sunday dinner. Innocuous threats of harm scattered the clan across the portal and out the door. I alone was left to witness the continuation of the litany of potential disasters.

It really didn't matter. We both knew I wasn't the guilty party. I never was. I inched my jolting legs back to my place of refuge. Instinctively, the nearest family member elevated me to safety, hesitating briefly in mid-air as my disobedient legs sought to coordinate in their place through the open back of the chair. My knees found the formed pouches they had previously occupied, warm and welcoming.

As the table was being transformed to prepare for the *past*, my eyes caught a glimpse of my sisters disappearing behind bare bushes. In the distance, the cadence echoed off the partially frozen ground amidst shrieks of joy. I proudly placed my neatly creased napkins and piles of freshly scratched cheese before me. Samples from the simmering pots aligned my works of art.

Eventually, I would come to embrace the inside looking out. Instead, I gripped the thickly buttered heel of fresh Italian bread as tenaciously as my *longing* to be pounding the unforgiving ground, and savored every morsel given for a job well done.

Psalm 63

O God you are my God—for you I long!

For you my soul is thirsting.

My body pines for you like a dry

    weary land without water.

So I gaze at you in the sanctuary to see

    your strength and your glory

For your love is better than life.

My lips will speak your praise.

So will I bless you all my life. In your

    name I will lift up my hands.

My soul shall be filled as with a banquet.

    My mouth shall praise you with joy.

On my bed I remember you. On you I muse

    through the night, for you have been my

    help, in the shadow of your wings

I rejoice, my soul clings to you.

Your right hand holds me fast.

(cf. Psalm 63)

O God,

How often have I begun to pray this Psalm and gotten no further than O God in either absolute awe or utter despair, before the Blessed Sacrament or while pacing some parking lot? O God, how often have I neglected to recognize the gift of faith in simply being able to cry out, O God, much less …

my God for whom I long

He, who is the source and object of our longing!

He, who calls us into being.

He, the Alpha and the Omega, in the "summons and the sending," in my choosing and being chosen … for whom I long.[101]

For you my soul is thirsting.

"You will look for me, he says in John, where I am going you cannot come. I must leave you for a little while" (cf. John 7: 34–36). As he reveals and conceals himself in this lifelong mystery of divine hide and seek, the very thought, feeling, and image of him hides infinitely more.[102]

Where what you do not know is all you know.[103]

> "As we learn to live with the restlessness of desire. [104] says St. Augustine

My body pines for you like a dry weary land without water.

I was blessed with the experience of a dry, weary land, while hitchhiking across the desert in July. My daughter of three months and I were without food or water. All that I owned was in a broken down car left behind. The temperature was 120° in the shade that day. I waited for the sun to set before proceeding across the hills to San Diego. It would have to be before dark as it might be snowing there. I rinsed out her pajamas with water from an old rusted faucet. I laid it on a large rock to dry. It was so hot that her last piece of protection against the elements literally caught fire!

"True love and prayer are learned in the moments when prayer becomes impossible and the heart has turned to stone," says Merton.[105]

I had $.35 in my pocket. "Freedom's just another word for nothing else to lose", sings Janis.[106] The sunset was as beautiful as I have ever seen that day.

So I gaze on you in the sanctuary to see your strength and your glory.

I can wait, I can watch. I can listen, I can in all things prepare a place for you to come into my soul, but you alone will bring it to fulfillment, when you alone are all that I see.

"Something happens," says Rudolf Otto, in speaking of the experience of the "mysterium tremendum."[107] Something happens to the one who gazes on him in the sanctuary to see his strength and his glory. But no one is quite able to say what that something is.

Von Balthasar tries, "Quietly without our knowing it an angel comes and nudges us on the shoulder, the gate flies open, and we walk out past the sleeping guards to freedom."[108] Something happens without our knowing it and we are led to pray with conviction,

For your love is better than life.

> Once there was a young monk in the forest monastery who went to the teacher and asked, "Master, I studied hard, learned all the sutras well, meditated diligently, and have been obedient in all things, but I long to know the truth. Please let me go to the mountain where I

shall either die or find that which I seek. It does not matter, for I would rather die than live not knowing." Realizing that the young monk was prepared for such solitude, the master gave him the permission he sought. So the young man packed up a few belongings tied onto the end of a stick over his shoulder and proceeded toward the mountain. As he was leaving the last village, he noticed an old man coming down. He thought, "Perhaps this old man knows something of which I seek. I will ask him, since it may be the last person I ever see." As he approached the old man, he told him the whole story of how hard he worked and how deeply he longed to see the truth, ending with, "Can you help me? Do you have any advice for me before I go?" (He did not realize, of course, that this was the famous Bodhisattva who appears to those ready for enlightenment.) The old man, who also carried his life's possessions upon his shoulder, looked at the young monk and—without a word—placed the bundle on the ground before him. In that moment, the young man leaped for joy! He understood in that simple act that the truth lies in the final letting go of all things. When he recovered from this magnificent experience, he said "Now what shall I do?" After all, he had this agenda prepared for the rest of his life. The old monk simply bent down and picked up his bundle and proceeded back to the marketplace.[109]

"You cannot know the truth, says Stephen Levine, you can only enter directly the moment in which truth resides." [110] To discover a love better than life, one must be prepared to die. Paul knew it. John Vianney knew it, too. "If only you knew how much God loves you, you would die for joy!" He meant die![111]

"He who climbed the mount of the Beatitudes must necessarily climb the mount of Calvary," says Sheen, "to practice what he preached."[112]

My lips will speak your praise, so will I bless you all my life. In your name I will lift up my hands. My soul shall be filled as with a banquet, my mouth shall praise you with joy!

On my bed I remember you ...

Metanoia has as much to do with remembering as longing. Emmanuel agrees. In answer to the question:

> How can there be such evil ... so much injustice ... how do we help?
>
> "You can primarily begin by offering yourself another word, another definition for evil. When one says evil, whatever it is you are trying to do something about is immediately cast outside your heart, and outside your heart nothing can be done. Renamed more accurately, ask why is there so much forgetting in the world, so

much unexpressed and unfulfilled longing. Verbalized that way the answer is
clearer, is it not? What to do? To love, to
love, to love. Become the loving teacher.
Be who you are in as much love as you
possess, as you have allowed yourself to
remember. Be that loving, remembering human being within the company of
the forgetter, and they will see your light
when they are ready and they will hear
you when they can and pray for them."[113]

On you I muse through the night, for you have
been my help. In the shadow of your wings I
rejoice. My soul clings to you; your right hand
holds me fast.

Sometimes when I muse through the night
before drifting off to sleep, I remember.

Sometimes I pray a short form of compline
using the ancient metta or loving-kindness
meditation.

God, come to my assistance, Lord, make haste to help me. Glory be to the father and the son and the holy spirit, Amen.

May you be happy.
May you be at peace.
May you know the oneness of all beings.
May you know love.
If there is anyone I have harmed
  this day, may I be forgiven *and*
  to myself, I forgive you.
If there is anyone who has
  hurt me, I forgive you.
May all beings, (praying for indi-
  viduals, groups, the church, the
  world etc.) be peaceful.
May all beings be happy.
May all beings be strong
  in mind and body.
May all beings know joy in the accep-
  tance of things just as they are.[114]

> Now, master let your servant go in peace,
> according to your word, for my eyes have
> seen your salvation, which you prepared
> in the sight of all the peoples, a light of
> revelation to the gentiles and the glory
> for your people Israel."
>
> (cf. Luke 2:29–32)

Glory be to the father and the son and the holy spirit, amen.

May the lord grant us a restful night, a peaceful death, and be with our absent brothers and sisters, amen.

Dear Jesus,

I love you from the fullness of a grateful heart bursting with joy. While still attempting to use words and "every attempt a different kind of failure," I surrender completely to you.[115] Now is the time. As a precious mosaic, you have pieced my life together. As a precious mosaic, you hold me in your hands. My responsibility is to gaze, only to gaze on the one for whom I live my life. Amen.

)

Loving

All Hallow's Eve

All Hallow's Eve of All Saints is the eve of All
Souls. How convenient for the merciless sisters
who reveled in enlightening little ones banished to
released time the Tuesday before Halloween. What
could be more disillusioning (or boring) than the
theological exegesis exposing the origin of jack-o-
lanterns and ghosts? It compares to none other than
dispelling the myth of Santa Claus to a seven-year-
old because "it's time." Time for what, no one can
tell except by divine revelation, it's just one more of
those obscurities, one more of life's cruelties. With
any luck, some entrusted soul (no pun intended)

would be complicit in sustaining the imagination for just a while longer.

In the meantime, the five Neri girls would impatiently hit the brisk air before dusk. Shuffling in close proximity from house to house, the Windmill St. rounds took no less than three hours. Windmill Hill extended a mere half mile from ledge to end. Nearly everyone in the neighborhood was related to one another. I never quite got who was a *cumbard* and who was a *padine,* but I'm sure the translations were sufficiently broad to encompass almost anyone who made wine in the cellar, grew tomatoes, spoke the same dialect, smelled like garlic, or wore black.

One such household at a time would complete the ritual of advancing the steamy masked horde of ghouls through the kitchen and past the plastic covered parlor in search of sufficient light. It was not until then that the query game could begin. Complete with "Oh mys" and "Aahs," there were always three guesses, and even though it was understood that the first two didn't count, we always pretended to be excited when our identity was finally revealed.

Since costumes were recycled amongst the clan each year, no contemplation was actually required, but what fun would that be? The threadbare legs approached the knees, the tattered tie had long since reached, and the sparkly stuff gave scarcely a hint of the proud skeleton it once had been. Yet, year after year, we donned our assigned character with glee. It wasn't until my elder sister elaborated on the gypsy costume she wore in "Fiddler on the Roof" that any of us realized that a costume did not have to come in a box.

There were few restrictions apart from being hit by a car. While costumes were economized, thankfully, candy bars were still whole and sampling was not only permissible, but unlimited. Nutrition and safety got very little press in those days. Paranoia had not permeated our *Leave it to Beaver* neighborhood. Fear of a razor blade showing up in an apple was still a few years off. There wasn't a presidential appointed committee to investigate children and obesity, and no one ever heard of trans fat, much less knew what it was.

Despite the nuns, we lived in a sheltered era. Save the scarcity of means, we lived in an abundant time. Though secluded by culture and religion, the inherent kinship surpassed any hint of isolation. Thus armed with *love,* the skeletons of yesteryear embrace the goblins of today and remember when.

"Expect everything, worry about nothing," says St Therese Lisieux. "Confidence and trust is a fundamental childhood attitude."[116]

It doesn't matter if we love God; the whole point is … God loves us. (cf 1John 4: 10)

As children, we just knew that.

> A woman struggling to be "good," but frustrated by her failure, asks Emmanuel, "How can I be more loving?" His reply, "You cannot instruct the heart to be lov-

ing. You can act loving, everyone can do that. But hearts do not open on command. You are commanding the child to behave and the child is attempting to behave. Rather, embrace yourself in your unlovingness and ask the child, why can you not love? Listen for the answer. You may be quite surprised at what you hear and gain a new respect for yourself. Moved to compassion for your own pain, you will then be more loving."[117]

To become more loving calls for a humble, listening heart which knows what it does not know and sees what is unknown. To become more loving calls us to stand still and ask permission to know the most universal, the most tremendous, the most mysterious of forces"[118]

To become more loving calls for forgetfulness of things created, remembrance of the Creator, and attention to that which is within.[119]

To become more loving calls us "to soar above transitory things, to be fond of solitude and silence, to be in the atmosphere of the Holy Spirit and respond with his inspirations.[120]

To become more loving calls us to not desire to do anything except that which is the will of God.

"Please call me by my true names so I can wake up", says Thich Nhat Hanh, "so the door of my heart can be left open, the door of compassion. "[121]

Dear Jesus,

It's New Years. A few candles, music, a loving-kindness meditation … we are like music not contained, bringing love without substance or form, bringing truth dancing before the world, pointing the way. This moment has come to matter more than what I will do with the rest of my life, because it *is* the rest of my life.

My prayer, to do the father's will, to give him glory; that is all. Amen.

Reconciling

I am stuck. I am stuck in a place between the mountain and the marketplace, in a place of sadness and regret. But the prodigal father came out to get me. With e.e. cummings I had proclaimed, "the eyes of my eyes see, the ears of my ears awake."[122] Now, I can only speak from my disconnectedness. I was unable to live out that which I have been told.

It seems everything once uncovered has pride as its root. Most words only reflect the pride that supports the ego that refuses to give in. Self-forgetfulness turns out to be self-indulgence. Endurance to bear the relentless awareness of sinfulness becomes impossible. I am used up and worn out, and I can't say "I'm sorry" or "I love you" anymore. Besides, how can I still believe that what I say is true when experience tells me it isn't in the same moment?

"A clean heart, create for me, O God," I pray, "let me be like you in all my ways." (cf Psalm 51:10.) In all my ways, Lord? Why do I pray for such things when most times I'd rather pretend that I'm deaf, lower my eyes, and look away? If only I could remain steadfast.

What appears humble isn't, and transformation is a much different process than I had once supposed. It has become increasingly clear to me that with all that I am and am not there is no possible way that whatever good he manages through me could ever be anything but his care and his grace. As a matter-of-fact, I only seem to complicate and interfere with a very simple directive. Be one with him as he is with the father. It is for this that he has made me. This is the challenge. As he continues to call me, he continues to bless my soul.

God offers the promise of freedom from the imprisonment of our ego where misery and hope collide. Von Balthasar's account of just such a conflict is riveting:

> "You lure me into a deadly adventure, saying you desire to comingle your breath with my very breathing. You are a beggar for love, but don't you see, we are made for measure and limits. You know nothing of measure, but I must maintain my boundaries and remember that you are God. When you threaten to grip my heart, if I say with all humility, "Lord go away from me, for I am a sinner," I can create distance. If I say, "I am not worthy that you should come under my roof, but leave the rest out," you will remain God. I will wash your feet, anoint your head, and adore you as when you were transfigured on the mountain, but please don't come down again. It is the religious thing to do, you know, to recognize the infinite, qualitative difference between God and the world".

By erecting a chapel somewhere in a snug corner, you will be preserved. I can visit you daily and pray the office. "It will be a sign of my faith. I will stand before God eye to eye when your unfathomable glance pierces me. And I will long for wholeness. These are dangerous moments and times of anguish. But your gaze remains. Sometimes, if I pray very hard I can pray you away. Consumed by words, there's less chance of hearing you. Sooner or later, I will get the framework of my spirituality to replace you. And then, then I will have peace. It cannot be otherwise, you know; creatures have their measure and limits. And when this finitude encounters your infinite love, there is a fear of being burst asunder. It is a pious error to think we long for the infinite. Experience contradicts it. Instead we lay down our peace offering and ask that you be satisfied with it. Please don't trespass my boundaries. You may over-wind the spring on the clock. Know that the measure by which I judge myself is a definite scale of perfection, which I have devised drawing on your clearly expressed prohibitions. I supplement those with voluntary works of love, so as not to hear your unclear and amorphous call to the undefined. My space is familiar to me, and only within can I know the world or even you. I do not long to go out of myself. By long association I have grown fond of this house of my suffering with all its shortcomings. I do not wish to be stripped down, but clothed over. You cannot exact the impossible feat that I should become a stranger to myself and at midnight like a thief climb out of my own window to a certain death."[123]

Please, please don't ask this of me.

T.S. Eliot describes the experience at the threshold of the unknown as being "in a dark wood on the edge of the grimpen menaced by monsters and fancy lights risking enchantment."[124]

The monsters and the enchantment are equally perilous. Perhaps the fancy lights are even more perilous. In either case it doesn't matter, because it will pass.

Jesus lifts us beyond our limited image of him again and again. We wait in a dark wood for his promise to return until he withdraws again that we might grow from impression to withholding to return in search of the inexhaustible mystery of God! That Tabor experience to which I held resolutely for far too long made it nearly impossible to continue in any direction.

Now, little by little, I yield to him, as little by little I see that his ways are not mine. I realize that I created an idol out of the image I fashioned for myself. This idol that I presumably melted and molded for him has not been his image at all. The likeness he offers me is that I may be who I am. In the journey toward wholeness, the very self I tried desperately to be rid of, has been, in fact, his highest gift to me.

The glory of God may be man fully alive, but the soul is afraid of dying and afraid of living in him at the same time. We are afraid to be with the one who has proven again and again to be all we need. The self hangs onto both the pain and the need! How silly we are in our stubbornness. It is a fight for survival. It won't give up easily. After all, this is the tangible proof that we exist, otherwise we are mere imagination, even less perhaps, and that scares me even more. The self continues to kick, holler, and scream. It will give up one day and, when it does, he will accompany me further into himself. Until then, I surrender and wait as I am able. That is all there is to do.

Thus, I found the courage to pray with Carlo Carretto,

> "Come then, death, come. I am waiting. You do not frighten me anymore; I no longer see you as a foe. I see you as my sister. I look you in the face. I understand you now. As you come towards me I tell you, held firm in your mighty hand, do with me as you will. Wholeheartedly, I say this to you, truthfully I say this to you, lovingly I say this to you, do with me

as you will. Accustom me to this extreme abandonment. Accustom me to this never ending adult kiss, to this never finished conversation. Accustom me little by little, by distributing my death through all the days of my life. Put it on my bread like ashes or sand that I may not live by bread alone. Put it in my house as something lacking, that I may never accept the limitations of the visible. Put it as insecurity in my security, that I may only be secure in him alone. Put it in the midst of my joy as a reminder, so that I may become used to being alone for that moment when I shall be alone with you."[125]

But God defies containment and the "hour" of my tryst with "death" had not come. My beckoning to go beyond my "measure and limits" simply rendered me helpless and oppressed. That which restrained me, plagued me. I realized later that passion leads to intimacy, then to fear of pain, and finally to fear of being utterly alone.

I pleaded for peace, or rather for relief. "But then you would not know true joy," he replied.

> "You will know very little until you get there. You will journey blind, but this way leads toward possession of what you have sought for in the wrong place. What do you know of the kind of suffering you must undergo on the way?"[126]

I met with my meditation teacher today. "I'm frightened," I said. "There's nothing left to hold on to. So much is illusion." "Can you gently let go of what you leave behind while embracing what lies before you?" he said. He captured the posture which nearly destroyed me. I was pushing away, while protecting against. Such clarity! Thank you.

"All things good and bad come and go," my grandmother used to say in Italian.

Suffering is wishing it were otherwise.

Dear Lord,

I find myself holding the breath of my thoughts, knowing you will bring to completion the good you have begun, knowing my heart, my mind, and my understanding are much too small. I know too that in a moment I will question and complicate the very word I hold this moment to be my reason for being. For so long, I have trembled on a distant shore, gazing into the abyss which separates us; for all too long. Eternal is your mercy from age to age. Lamb of God, you take away the sins of the world, speak but the word, and I shall be healed. Amen

Awakening

"Eyes Have Not Seen, and Ears Have Not Heard" (cf. 1Corinthians 2: 9)

The air was warm and sticky. I noticed a faint mist rising just above the irregular surface from where I lay on the stony asphalt. There was a piercing pain at the back of my head; whether it was mist or blood that moistened the nape of my neck was difficult to distinguish. My focus was rather fixed on the paralyzing glare of the oncoming headlights directly in front of me. Time as I knew it stood still. I became absorbed in one interminable moment when that which appeared inevitable seemed strangely okay. It's never been clear to me what happened next. The luminous, concentric beams merged until the muddied pieces of splintered treads etched its tracks in my memory forever.

It was the sting of tears washing over minor cuts and bruises on my face that awakened me. I was lying on a hard, paper-covered table alone, filled with questions and confusion. Who saved my life? How did I get here? Aloof and preoccupied, the occasional health care worker who entered the room was less than interested in my mysterious arrival. I could only recall the brush of air disturbed by whirling treads.

This experience was easier to forget than grasp until some years later when I found myself on a cold steel table consumed by pain and fear. A crowd of health care providers anxiously hovered while inquiries flew. "Where's the father? Who will decide between baby and mother?"

"He isn't here," I retorted, surprised the lucidity of my voice went unnoticed.

"Save my baby, of course!" Why in the world would that even be a question? Why was everyone so frantic? More importantly, why weren't they listening? Suddenly, I was struck by a shattering clarity. Instruments clanged with incisive tones. My vantage changed indiscernibly to the far right corner of the room. There "I" was looming above the clamor. Any effort to comfort the crowd, who by this time were blaming each other for my loss, was futile. "It's okay, really. It's okay. It's no one's fault," but my pleading fell on deaf ears.

The group below began focusing on the remaining life, desperate not to feel liable for two lives in one day. Then, my attention was drawn as if by a powerful magnet to a light, more by its brightness than its glare. I felt stilled more than paralyzed, by a penetrating sense of familiarity, oddly like returning home. The light, the stillness, the gaze united, whether it was a voice or a thought was not clear. I only know that I was offered a choice. Did I want to go home (toward the light) or go back? Instantaneously, "Home, of course," diffused immeasurable space followed just as quickly by a less penetrating whisper. "But who will care for my baby?" My attention had turned to the lifeless form below. Torn by that which was beyond comprehension and my responsibility to this child seemed to be the answer in itself. The decision was made. What happened next is less intelligible. The room was quieter now. I heard Apgar three, a faint cry, then nothing until I awoke two days later grasping cold metal rails alone.

While language often betrays the inexplicable, I submit to the poets and prophets who have mastered profound simplicity.

> "We are placed in this world for a little while that we might learn to bear the beams of love." Wm. Blake[127]

That which has been written again and again for our deaf ears to hear, placed before us again and again for our blind eyes to see, has tugged at our hearts for years only to be qualified and rejected. How can one ever reproduce in pictures, sound or word the love this God holds in his heart for each of us? I think my heart will break.

Life, though, is filled with "ten thousand joys and ten thousand sorrows;" from Tabor to Calvary and back to resurrection.[128] After the plunge into his loving hands, which we cannot begin to understand, after the struggle to hang onto who knows what, when there is no further violence to fear because death itself "has dealt its fiercest blow and lost," he comes.[129] "As a small, still voice," he comes (1 Kings 19:12). Without words we reach to touch his garment. Without words he heals our wounds. In fear and disbelief, we tremble to realize that he truly is the Son of God.

It is not coincidental that I now have no energy of my own to alter this course. All that has come before is meaningless. All that I learned in years previous largely wasted. I surrender because there is nothing left to do. It bears no affirmation, I assure you. I let it be with complete abandon. I allowed my spirit to be surrounded by the God of hosts who, in his everlasting mercy, gives me his grace and his love. His grace and love is all I need.

- What happens next? I don't know.

- What's different? Everything.

- What do I think about all this? Absolutely nothing.

- What do I discern from all this? There is actually nothing in the world of which he is not a part, absolutely nothing.

Lift, place, step. I made my way to the front of the meditation hall where the altar, adorned with flowers from the gardens surrounding the monastery, held a beautifully carved statue of Buddha. I was still wrapped in a thin, soft shawl, but it provided little comfort. A solid, heavy presence in the center of my chest prevailed—obscure yet inescapable. I made my way across the main dining room. Seeking solace, I ascended the stairs leading through the annex to my enclosure with this nebulous mass rising and falling with each passing breath. Step, step, intention, reach; the thud of the door echoed softly through the vacant corridor.

As if the final inaudible click of the door handle was itself permission, this pain became more discernable and demanded my attention. I sat at the edge of the simple wooden bed frame and leaned forward in anguish. I began to sob. Time was measured in moments. A cushion had been created by my arms folded tightly across my chest as the assault danced about. My tears bathed the small hairs on my arms before falling onto my lap which had steadied itself with the gentleness of a begging bowl. I cannot recall a more penetrating *scream!* I cannot imagine surviving greater intensity than this; all in deafening silence. Oddly, unfamiliar faces began to stream before me in an endless parade. It was incomprehensible and irrational.

Eventually, the gasp that had paralyzed me, released me. As I turned, I was struck by three trees framed by the open window. One was young and tender, one lay partially decayed on the forest floor, the other stood tall.

Yes, death is not personal. It just is. Everything lives and everything dies. It is a matter of course.

Later, a small group purported to be experienced meditators gathered in guru alley for an assigned check-in with the teacher. Each made their way into the room seeking either the most or the least comfortable space which was sure to disturb the depth of samahdi or concentration which had accumulated in days previous. I have never quite understood why this group is distinguished from the beginners, but then I have never been a fan of group meetings.

Nevertheless, it was my turn, so I recounted the experience briefly and asked, "What was that?" I was certain that somewhere in the volumes of Buddhist psychology and meditation there was a simple explanation for this clearly confusing experience that still vibrated within me. "I don't know," he replied. I cannot recall the speculation that followed. In the recounting, I had already betrayed the actual experience, which in itself was answer enough.

What was that? I had asked. The journey toward selflessness has been a difficult and dangerous one. Whether it is to the Buddhist void or the self-forgotten toward self-annihilation or union with the living God. Labels are meaningless. The self that I thought I knew no longer exists. Nothing is familiar.

"I peered into the water today; no one was there," I wrote. What I did not write was, "Fear was conspicuously absent." The ego deflates like a pin in a hot air balloon, but not before its time.

> Grace is ever-present
> We are simply human,
> simply human
> no more, no less
> divine only in him
> drowned in sorrow
> can't go back
> this breath please
> he has died, once for all
> that we might live!

There is no prescription leading to this place and no prescription leading from it.[130] Selflessness is not the desire to not be, says Roberts. "That which is annihilated is the knowing of the thought and feeling of self not in God." So that's what John meant when he said, " ... from the fullness of a grateful heart, he rejoices that he is and at the same time desires unceasingly to be freed from the knowing and feeling of this being."[131]

This place, which I feared for so long, this oneness within and without at the same time, for which I have no frame of reference, unspectacular and impermanent, in moment to moment, either self-fulfilled or self-less, the living God continues to teach my soul. So, after years of inward movement, I began years of an outward movement, at peace with this prayer:

"luminous tendril of celestial wish ... through twilight's mystery made flesh ... teach disappearing also me the keen illimitable secret of begin."

—e.e. cummings[132]

Dear Jesus,

It has been a day marked by loose ends and blessings. Grace lifts my eyes to you; I hear you in the breath of life around me. As bread blessed and broken, we recognize you, as from dream through deception, what's possible emerges.

"I am who am." You are, we are empty vessels, channels of your love. (Exodus 3:14). You are the potter, we the clay, (cf Isaiah 64:7) into being from the stillness, we now pray "my soul does proclaim the greatness of the Lord; my spirit rejoices in you" (Luke1:46), God my Savior. Amen

One day, while attempting to meditate, I encountered a spider on the nearby radiator. The spider was more interesting than the metta phrases this sitting, so I stopped and watched as the frenetic pace became an attempt to climb. "May you be safe and protected … " I continued the blessings, "May you find peace in acceptance of just who you are." Metta came easily for this creature. No surprise. Nature has been my anchor since the start. He kept trying to climb, falling to safety shortly thereafter again and again. He reached millimeter heights over previous efforts, which sounds a lot like my practice.

My joyful interest intensified and then it happened. He climbed ever so far up the wall to where and why I did not know, I only felt his steadfastness with such compassion. Ugh! He fell. My heart fell with him. What a disappointment. I wanted him to succeed because that is what he seemed to want. I rooted for him: "You can do it, come on, you can do it." But he couldn't do it. He fell, not physically hurt, but he did not try again. He came to the end of the heater and disappeared. A lifetime changes in the walk from here to there; then it is gone. I felt a certain emptiness and a certain familiarity. Equanimity comes in the acceptance (and letting go) of things just as they are one moment at a time.

Joseph leaned forward from his place at the front of the meditation hall and smiled. "I am going to tell you the secret of Nirvana!" he said. "Ready? There is no separateness." He paused then asked,

"Did anyone get enlightened?" A murmur of laughter swept across the meditation hall. "Well then," he said, settling back onto his cushion in his forever perfect pose, "shall we meditate?"

Thirty years later and the driveway is neatly paved now. The austerity of a thin slab of foam for a bed has been replaced through the generosity of benefactors with simply furnished cells. The aroma of delicious vegetarian cooking replaces the pungent smell of unfamiliar spices from a far-off land.

After all, this is not a forest monastery in Burma. I never trekked thousands of miles across rough terrain to join courageous seekers from the West. Nor have I fallen ill from disease, mosquitos, or unclean water. As it turns out, it is not the necessary evil I once thought it was. A moment here, a moment there, West or East, is still just a moment; nothing to earn. The truth prevails in the acceptance of gift and the task of letting go; or rather *be,* says Jon Kabat-Zinn.[133] With this in-breath and this out-breath, the hunter becomes the warrior, and the warrior discovers all in all. No big deal.

"With this he closed his eyes to descend into darkness, and when he opened them the separation had been removed. It was the world which had always existed in his heart but which only begins to beat the moment one beats in union with it," says Auguste, in *Smile at the Foot of the Ladder*.[134]

While it is an impossible task, I will attempt to relate an experience of oneness. Yes, we are connected—letters on paper to make words non-describable of the fact that one is in all and all is in one. The trees ahead and the creatures beneath them know much more than I of the immensity of the cosmos to which we belong.

> One sitting at a time
> thirty years in one lifetime later
> no matter
> no difference
> a moment explodes revealing the universe
>   in a single "grain of sand ... a flower"[135]
> it's true

the trees find you ... if you let them
that is also true
the ache in my left knee pulsates,
  comes, goes, and comes again like
  a warm blanket this time, as
the lawnmower hums across the
  lawn like a badly tuned organ
unable to drown out the bellows
  emitting from the nearby trees
through the dance of the
  breeze off my cheek
one moment
one moment
no matter
no difference
just is

"A million ages in the past before the world had yet begun I danced in the garden all alone and I and me were one. The years have come, the years have gone with much to know and do, the garden gate is closed to us while I and me are two. The garden walls are crumbling now

> as do gives way to be and Yahweh reaches
> to enfold as I blend into me."[136]

How could one ever hope to express the gratitude owed to countless persons who bring us such teachings; Buddhist or Christian. We are all "enlightened". We have always known that. Each moment offers the opportunity to step into now; shed the confines of our narrow sense of self, and experience the love which holds all beings together around this container, his vessel, emptied and receptive to be his conduit in the world. All prayer, all action, all thought, either contributes to the force of nature or destroys it. The onus of the responsibility lies in the practice of the presence of this moment we call now.

> May all beings be safe and protected.
> May all beings be peaceful.
> May all beings be strong
>   in mind and body.
> May all beings share in the joy of accep-
>   tance of things just as they are.

A Rabbi spent years in solitude meditating on the mystery of the divine in all things ... a feeble approximation of what he had discovered was written in books. He later remarked, "I had hoped to help but perhaps I should not have spoken at all." [137]

The end.

Apendix 1

Biography of Jean-Baptiste-Marie Vianney

Jean-Baptiste entered the seminary in 1812 at Verrieres but failed to pass the examinations for entrance to the seminary proper. He later succeeded, and on 13 August, 1815, he was ordained a priest. His difficulties seem to have been, in theory, as distinct from practice—a lack accounted for by the meagerness of his early schooling, the advanced age at which he began to study, the fact that he was not of more than average intelligence, and that he was far advanced in spiritual science and in the practice of virtue long before he came to study it in the abstract. In 1818 Vianney was made parish priest of Ars, a village not very far from Lyons. It was in the exercise of the functions of the parish priest in this remote French hamlet that as the "Curé d'Ars" he became known throughout France and the Christian world.

The chief labor of the Curé d'Ars was the direction of souls. He had not been long at Ars when people began coming to him from other parishes, then from distant places, then from all parts of France, and, finally, from other countries. During the last ten years of his life, he spent sixteen to eighteen hours a day in the confessional. His advice was sought by bishops, priests, religious young men and women in doubt as to their vocation, sinners, persons in all sorts of difficulties, and the sick. His direction was characterized by common sense, remarkable insight, and supernatural knowledge. His instructions were simple in language, full of imagery drawn from daily life, and breathing faith in the love of God, which was his life principle. He infused this love as much by his manner and appearance as by his words, for, at the last, his voice was almost inaudible.

Miracles regarding money for his charities, supernatural knowledge, and healing the sick—especially children—have been attributed to him.

The greatest miracle of all was his life. He practiced mortification and labored incessantly with unfailing humility, gentleness, patience, and cheerfulness until he was more than seventy-three years old.

On 3 October, 1874 Jean-Baptiste-Marie Vianney was proclaimed Venerable by Pius IX and on 8 January, 1905, he was enrolled among the Blessed. Pope Pius X proposed him as a model to the parochial clergy.

(Note: In 1925, Pope Pius XI canonized him. His feast is kept on 4 August.)[138]

Appendix 2

Explanation of Icon by Msgr. Anthony LaFemina

The mediator's task is to interpose between parties as equal friend of each, especially to effect reconciliation. Since Jesus Messiah is simultaneously true God and true Man, he can be the only mediator—the unique bridge—between God and mankind.

Though not every mediator is a priest, the priest is always a mediator. The priestly character broadens the mediator's office. The Epistle to the Hebrews specifies that the Lord Jesus is a priest: "We have a great high priest who has passed through the heavens, Jesus, the Son of God" (Heb. 4:14).

The Father anointed him eternal high priest from the first moment of his conception in the womb of the blessed Virgin Mary, by reason of his singular grace of the union of his divine and human natures in his divine person. The epistle to the Hebrews explains Jesus Messiah as priest by stating that he "is taken from among men and made their representative before God to offer gifts and sacrifices for sins" (Heb. 5:1).

Because our Savior came to restore a broken union between God and mankind, his sacerdotal activity necessarily has the character of atonement. His priestly mediation is twofold: ascending and descending. The Lord achieves his ascending mediation in offering the supreme sacrifice of his earthly life, together with the prayers and works of his church. He offers these for his Father's glory and for the life of the world through the forgiveness of sins.

Jesus accomplishes his descending mediation by bestowing the divine gifts of God's teaching and grace upon mankind. "Sacerdos," the Latin word for priest, means precisely "giving sacred things" (sacra dans).

The Priesthood of All Believers

While the Lord Jesus is the sole priest of the new covenant, he made all members of his church share by grace in his unique priesthood. His church is "a kingdom of priests for his God and Father" (Rev 1:6; cf. 1 Peter 2:5, 9).

These priests—both men and women, adults and children—are the "authentic worshippers" who "worship the Father in Spirit and truth" (John 4:23). The priesthood of all the faithful is called the Baptismal or Common priesthood. The faithful receive this priestly consecration with the sacraments of Baptism and Confirmation and exercise it by taking part in Christian worship "in Spirit and truth," by the reception of the other sacraments, and by the witness of their holy, prayerful and courageously virtuous lives in accord with their particular vocations (cf. Catechism of the Catholic Church, n. 1546; Lumen Gentium, 10).

Ministerial Priesthood—Holy Orders

The Lord Jesus also wills to share his priesthood with his church in another way, through the valid reception of the Sacrament of Holy Orders. This special priesthood is called the ministerial priesthood. The Lord established this particular sharing in his priesthood as a service to the common priesthood since it is directed to the unfolding of the faithful's baptismal grace and to enable them to offer their own "spiritual sacrifices" (1 Peter 2:5) in authentic worship of the Father in union with his own sacrifice (PO, n. 2). Thus, through the instrumentality of the ministerial priest, Christ himself makes his members an eternal gift to the Father (cf. 1 Peter 3:18).

The ministerial priesthood has two degrees: the episcopacy (bishops) and the presbyterate (priests) (CCC, n. 1554). This ministerial sharing in the Lord's unique priesthood is the means by which he continually builds up and leads his church. The ministerial priesthood differs not only in degree but also in essence from the common priesthood because it confers special powers and correlative duties upon bishops and priests. Whether bishops or priests, however, ministerial priests exercise the supreme degree of their sacred functions in the same way: by celebrating the Eucharist (LG, n. 28).

For this reason, the icon presents the ministerial priest during this celebration. The ministerial priest's life and mission are so linked to the Eucharistic sacrifice that he is called to become completely one with it in order to become, himself, a sacrifice of praise (John Paul II, L'Osservatore Romano, July 20, 2001).

The Priestly Sacrifice

The sacrifice of Calvary is always present in heaven and ceaselessly celebrated there by the church triumphant. This sacrifice's heavenly presence is indicated in the icon by the living blood and water gushing forth from the heart of the Savior. However, by the Lord's express will and command, his eternalized sacrifice is also made present on earth by the Eucharistic celebration through the instrumentality of the ministerial priesthood.

The Eucharistic sacrifice joins as one the church militant with the church triumphant in the unique sacrifice of both their liturgies. The instrumentality of the priest in making this sacrifice present on earth is illustrated in the icon by the blood and water coming from Christ's side and being offered to the eternal father by the hand of the priest. The ministerial priesthood is so connected to the Eucharist that this priesthood cannot be correctly contemplated outside of the Eucharistic mystery. Only through and in the measure of an authentic knowledge of the Eucharist can the supernatural nature of the ministerial priesthood be sufficiently grasped.

The Holy Spirit is pictured in the icon above the priest since the priest brings about the Eucharist (sacrifice—sacrament—presence) through the power of the Spirit. Our Lord instituted his ministerial priesthood for the purpose of realizing the new worship "in Spirit and truth" about which he spoke to the Samaritan woman (John 4:19–24). The icon attempts to illustrate what mystically takes place in this worship during the only part of the Eucharistic celebration wherein Christ personally intervenes: the consecration of the mass.

At that time the ministerial priest, fulfilling the express command of Christ ("Do this in memory of me"), acts, not in the name of Christ nor in his place, but in the Person of Christ— "This is my body my blood." The priest speaks the consecratory words "in specific sacramental identification with the eternal high priest who is the Author and Subject of this sacrifice, a sacrifice in which, in truth, nobody can take his place" (*Dominicæ Cenæ*, n. 8).

In celebrating the Holy sacrifice, the priest is sacramentally and wondrously brought into the most profound sacredness of Christ's person and made part of it. This sacramental identification with the eternal high priest enables the ministerial priest, as the Lord's consecrated instrument, to lend the Lord his intelligence, will, voice, and hands so as to offer through his very ministry the sacrifice of redemption to the Father.

The ministerial priest is "the sacramental representation of Christ the Head and Shepherd" (John Paul II, *L'OR,* Dec. 5, 2001). This is to say that the ministerial priest is a divinely written icon of Christ the priest (cf. CCC, n. 1142). His sacramental identification with the eternal high priest is indicated in the icon by the Greek Letters "IC" (Jesus) and "XC" (Christ) on the extremities of the priest's stole. These letters are used in icons to identify only the person of the Lord Jesus.

Ascending Mediation

In his ascending mediation, the ministerial priest offers to the heavenly Father, together with the Lord's unique sacrifice, the prayers and sacrifices of God's people that are symbolized by the smoking golden thurible of fragrant incense in the priest's hand (cf. Ps 141:2; Rev 5:8; 8:3,4). There, through a personal life of prayer and penance united with the sacrifice he offers, he entreats the Father's mercy for himself and all those souls whom God has providentially confided to his priestly vocation. It is the Lord's will that the ministerial priest, while offering the Eucharistic sacrifice, carries within his heart the prayers and sacrifices of all God's people before the throne of God.

Descending Mediation: Mercy, Love

In the exercise of his descending mediation the ministerial priest distributes the sacred gifts of the heavenly Father's merciful love. The ministerial priest is the instrumental cause of the production of the supernatural effects of those sacraments that require his priestly character for their administration. There at the throne of mercy the priest obtains graces that accrue to the universal church and other graces to be transmitted during the exercise of his ministry in the administration of the sacraments, in blessing, praying, preaching, teaching, counseling, caring, etc.

The icon illustrates the nature of the ministerial priest's descending mediation by the blood and water gushing from the side of Christ, which, when leaving the hand of the priest, become red and white rays that flow down upon the world below. These rays are inspired by the writings about divine mercy of Saint Faustina Kowalska of the most blessed sacrament, the first canonized saint of the present millennium.

Pope John Paul II gives a basic notion of mercy, whether divine or human, in his Encyclical, Dives in misericordia, when he teaches that love must condition justice so that justice may serve love.

Love is transformed into mercy when it is necessary to go beyond the norm of justice. The relationship between justice and love is manifested precisely in mercy. And thus, God mercifully deals with sinful humanity in the gift of his only Son, in whom He gives us every other blessing. The descending mediation of the ministerial priest involves the distribution of all those gifts coming, precisely, from our Father, who is infinite love and mercy.

The rays signifying God's merciful gifts are depicted in the icon by the red and white rays that come from the blood and water of the Lord's side flowing into the hand of the ministerial priest. Once in the hand of the priest, the blood and water become the red and white rays of divine mercy. The red rays signify the blood of our Savior that is the undeniable proof of the heavenly Father's merciful love for all persons without exception. The red rays also signify the Eucharist as the life and nourishment of souls.

The white rays indicate the Holy Spirit, who makes souls holy and pleasing to God in a special way through Holy Mass and all the sacraments, but especially through the forgiveness of sin in the sacraments of Baptism and Reconciliation (Penance).

Pope John Paul II teaches that because the priest is the minister of Christ's sacrifice and of his mercy, the priest is indissolubly bound up with the two sacraments of the Eucharist and Reconciliation (L'OR, July 20, 2001).

Saint Paul regarded himself as a servant of Christ and steward of the mysteries of God (1 Cor. 4:1). He also affirmed that he possessed his ministry through God's mercy (2 Cor. 4:1). In this vein the congregation for the clergy proclaims to every priest: "Priest of God, you embody the Mystery of Mercy!"

In fact, the ministerial priesthood is God's merciful gift because it is a privileged channel of his merciful love, not only for the church, but also for the entire human race. The ministerial priesthood brings mankind the inestimable gifts of infinite mercy. They are inestimable because "without mercy souls become as parched land on which the desert relentlessly encroaches, devouring hope, and the human heart resembles a lonely and dark cave" (Congregation for the Clergy, May 13, 2001).

God is infinite mercy, and he desires that we practice mercy (Mt 9:13; Hosea 6:6). In the

Eucharistic sacrifice, the priest presents to all mankind both the source of the infinite mercy that God is, and the school of the mercy that God desires we practice in our lives.

The Priest Brings Good News

The priest is portrayed in the icon with golden shoes decorated with precious stones to reflect the words of Saint Paul: "How beautiful are the feet of those who announce good news" (Romans 10:15; cf. Is 52:7). It is precisely God's mercy that the priest brings to mankind on behalf of the church in his service of evangelization. "To evangelize" means "to announce good news," and this good news is concretized in the person of Jesus Messiah, who is God's infinite mercy incarnate. However, in bringing the Lord Jesus to mankind, the priest, as minister of his church, must also bring the church with him. Jesus is indissolubly espoused to his church and is its head as any head is part of its body. If evangelization is to be authentic, the evangelizer must keep in mind that the Catholic church is

God's universal sign of salvation. This is to say the church is the sign of Jesus Christ himself, who is, in person, our salvation.

In the icon the seraphic figures of the four evangelists come forth from the throne of God (Ezk. 1:5–7,9,10,12; Rev. 4:6–8). Only persons on earth need evangelization, and the ministerial priests carry out this evangelization as their "priestly service of the gospel of God" (Romans 15:16). The ministerial priest fulfills his teaching office as part of his descending mediation and at the explicit command of the Lord Jesus: "Go, therefore, and make disciples of all nations, baptizing them in the name of the Father, and of the Son, and of the Holy Spirit, teaching them to observe all that I have commanded you. And behold, I am with you always, until the end of the world" (Mt. 28:19, 20).

Pope John Paul II teaches that "the priest is not the man of his own personal initiatives; he is the minister of the Gospel in the name of the Church. His apostolic activity takes its origin from the church and returns to the Church" (*L'OR,* May 16, 2001).[139]

Endnotes

1   Address of His Holiness Benedict XVI to the Members of
    the Congregation for the Clergy on the Occasion of their
    Plenary Assembly at Consistory Hall on March 16, 2009,
    www.vatican.va/holy_father/benedict_xvi/speeches/2009/
    march/documents/hf_ben-xvi_spe_20090316_plenaria-
    clero_en.html(April 15, 2010)

2   Ade Bethune, St. John Vianney (St. Paul, MN: College of
    St. Catherine, 1986) ABC6320

3   Women for Faith and Family, wf-f.org/Priests-prayer.html

4   Women for Faith and Family, wf-f.org/Priests-prayer.html

Beginning

5   Cardinal Basil Hume O.S.B., Searching for God (New York: Ampleforth Abbey Press,2002), 192.

6   ——Searching for God, 210.

7   A.W.Tozer, The Pursuit of God; Finding the Divine in the Everyday(Peabody, MA: Christian Pubications, 1993), 34.

8   Thomas Ryan, Prayer of Heart and Body: Meditation and Yoga as Christian Spiritual Practice (New York: The Missionary Society of St. Paul the Apostle, 1995), 108.

9   Lao Tsu and Gia-Fu Fing, Jane English (translators), Tao te Ching (New York: Knopf Doubleday Group, 1989), 64.

10 Bertrand Russell,
    History of Western Philosophy (Bulwell Lane, Basford Nottingham, NG6 0BT: Bertrand Russell Peace Foundation Ltd., 1996), 352.

11 Attributed to poetry by Margaret McGillvray

12 Dorothy Berkley Phillips, The Choice is Always Ours (University of California: Re-quest Books, 1982), 49.

Growing

13 Rainer Maria Rilke and Reginald Snell, Letters to a Young Poet (New York: Dover Publications, 2002), 30.

14 H.vander Looy, Rule for a New Brother (Springfield Illinois: Templegate Publishers, 1976), 32.

15 Robert L. Short, The Gospel According to Peanuts (Kentucky: Westminster John Knox Press, 2003), 103.

16 Clyde Kilby, ed., A Mind Awake; An Anthology of C.S.Lewis Letters to Malcolm, ch. 14 (Florida: Harcourt C.S. Lewis, PTE Ltd., 1968), 240.

17 Anthony Padovano, Free to be Faithful (Paramus, New Jersey: Paulist Press, 1972), 21.

18 Colman McCarthy, Inner Companions (California.: Acropolis, 1975), 171.

19 H.vander Looy, Rule for a New Brother (Springfield Illinois: Templegate Publishers, 1976), 64.

20 Rainer Maria Rilke and Reginald Snell, Letters to a Young Poet (New York: Dover Publications, 2002), 36.

21 Anthony Padovano, Free to be Faithful (Paramus, New Jersey: Paulist Press, 1972), 89.

22   Mother Teresa, Words to Love By (Indiana: Ave Maria
     Press, 1985), 47.

23   T. S .Eliot, The Complete Poems and Plays: 1909 -1950
     (Orlando, Florida: Harcourt Brace and Co., 1980), 198–201.

24   Michele McDonald, Dharma Talk, Retreat, June 2009.

25   Jack Kornfield and Christina Feldman, ed., Soul Food: Sto-
     ries to Nourish the Spirit and the Heart (New York: Harper
     Colllins Publishers, 1996), 45.

26   Michele McDonald, Dharma talk, Retreat June 2009.

27   Glenn Pease, Matthew 17: 1–13: Commentary (When the
     Son Glowed like the Sun, October 20, 2009), Chapter 4: 1.
     www.scribd.com/doc/21345199/

28   Unknown

Befriending

29   Michael Scott Peck, The Road Less Traveled and Beyond
     Spiritual Growth in an Age of Anxiety (New York: Touch-
     stone, 1998), 148.

30   John S. Dunne, The Reasons of the Heart: A Journey into
     Solitude and Back Again into the Human Circle (New

York: Macmillan Press, 1978), 38.

31   Annie Dillard, Teaching a Stone to Talk: Expeditions and Encounters (New York: Harper and Row, 1988), 19.

32   Unknown

33   Unknown

34   Shel Silverstein, The Giving Tree (New York: Harper Collins, 1992)

35   ———- Lafcadio, The Lion Who Shot Back (New York: Harper Collins, 1963)

36   C.S.Lewis, The Four Loves (New York: Harcourt Books, 1968), 16.

37   ———-The Four Loves, 101.

38   Frederick Franck, trans., Chuang Tzu, The Book of Angelus Silesius (Santa Fe, New Mexico: Bear and Co., Inc.), 101.

39   John Donne,Time and Myth (University of Michigan: University of Notre Dame Press, 1975) 103.

40   Plato, trans. .by G.M. Grube, The Republic (Indiannapolis, Indiana: Hackett, 1992) 5–10.

41   The Real Meaning of Life and Human Existence, new age spirituality © abracad 2004

www.new-age-spirituality.com/meanlife.html

42   Gary P.Hall, Autonomy and Surrender; Solitude and Inti-
     macy.www.thomasmertonsociety.org/hall.htm

43   Kahil Gibran, The Prophet (New York: Alfred A. Knopf, 91st
     ed., 1973), 12.

44   Unknown

Suffering

45   Attributed to a Buddhist monk

46   Basil Hume, In Praise of Benedict (Petersham, MA., St.
     Bede's Publications, 1981), 52

47   Fulton Sheen, Life of Christ (New York: Sheed and Ward,
     1958), 441–442.

48   Peter Boume, St Teresa's Castle of the Soul: A Study of the
     Interior Castle (California: Wenzel Press, 1995), 14.

49   Pope John Paul II/ Oct. 15, Congregation for the Clergy
     L'Osservatore Romano www.sjbrcc.net/jp2prc.html

50   Rowan Williams, Desmond Tutu and Lawrence Freeman,
     Where God Happens; Discovering God in One Another
     (Boston, Massachusetts: New Seeds Books, 2005), 138.

51   Anthony Padovano, Free to be Faithful (Paramus, New Jersey: Paulist Press, 1972), 70.

52   ———-,Free to be Faithful, 35.

53   ———-,Free to be Faithful, 47.

54   Reinhold Niebuhr, Serenity Prayer, http://www.thevoiceforlove.com/serenity-prayer.html

55   Robert L. Short, The Gospel According to Peanuts (Louisville, Kentucky: Westminster John Knox Press, 1965), 38.

56   John Henry Newman, Sermon 1: The Philosophical Temper First Enjoyed by the Gospel (Oxford University: Sermon 1, The National Institute for Newman Studies, 1826) www.newmanreader.org/works/oxford/sermon

57   T.S. Eliot, The Complete Poems and Plays; 1909–1950 (Orlando, Florida: Harcourt Brace and Co., 1980), 127.

58   Rainer Maria Rilke and Reginald Snell, Letters to a Young Poet (New York: Dover Publications, 2002), 40.

Reconciling

59   Johnston, W. ed. *The cloud of unknowing and The book of privy counselling* (New York: Image Books, 1973), 156.

60   Wilkie Au, By Way of the Heart: Toward a Holistic Spiritual Christian Spirituality (New Jersey: Paulist Press, 1989) 196.

61   Thich Nhat Hanh, Call Me by My True Names; The Collected Poems of Thich Nhat Hanh(California: Parallax Press,1999), 72.

62   Thomas Merton, Thoughts in Solitude (New York: Farrar, Straus, and Giroux, 1999), part 2, chapter 2.

63   J.L. Dawson, Peter Holland, David McKitterick, Thomas Stearns Eliot, A Concordance to the Complete Poems and Plays of T.S. Eliot (New York: Cornell University Press, 1995), 830.

64   Madeleine L'Engle, Walking on Water; Reflections on Faith and Art (New York: North Point Press, 1980) 134.

65   Robert L. Short, The Gospel According to Peanuts (Kentucky: Westminster John Knox Press, 2003)

66 John Peter Lange D.D., Philip Schaff D.D., ed., Volume 5, A Commentary on the Holy Scriptures (New York: Scribners, 1877), 312.

67 Thomas Merton, M. Basil Pennington, Thomas Merton; I Have Seen What I Was Looking For: Selected Spiritual Writings (New York: New City Press, 2005), 115.

68 Thomas Merton, Thoughts in Solitude (New York: Farrar, Straus and Giroux, 1999), 80.

69 Benjamin Hoff, The Tao of Pooh (New York: E.P. Dutton, 1982), 146.

70 Anthony Padovano, Free to be Faithful (Paramus, New Jersey: Paulist Press, 1972), 57.

71 H.vander Looy, Rule for a New Brother (Springfield Illinois: Templegate Publishers, 1976), 29.

72 Jack Kornfield, The Wise Heart (New York: Bantam Books, 2009), 91.

73 Hans Urs von Balthasar, Heart of the World (San Francisco: Liturgical Press, 1979), 72.

74 Henri Nouwen, Life of the Beloved; Spiritual Living in a Secular World (New York: Crossroad Publishing Co., 1992), 82–85.

Awakening

75 Hans Urs von Balthasar, Heart of the World (San Francisco: Liturgical Press, 1979), 215

76 Karl Rahner, trans. and foreword by James M. Demske, SJ, Encounters with Silence (South Bend, Indiana: St. Augustine's Press , 1999), 67.

77 Michele McDonald, Dharma talk, Retreat, June 2008.

78 William Barclay, The Gospel of Matthew (Kentucky: Westminster John Knox Press, 2001), 190.

79 William Davenport Adams, Dictionary of English Literature; Being a Comprehensive Guide to English Authors and their Works (Detroit: re-published by Gale Research Co., 1966), 151.

80 Jack Kornfield, Dharma talk, attributed to Steven Levine, Retreat, December 1981.

PART II—A Journey of Faith in Prayer and Meditation

81   John W. De Gruchy, Confessions of a Christian Humanist (Fortress Press, 2006), 22.

82   St. John of the Cross and Kathleen Jones, The Poems of St. John of the Cross (New York: Burns and Oates, 2001), 12.

83   H.vander Looy, Rule for a New Brother (Springfield Illinois: Templegate Publishers, 1976), 63.

84   Carlos Casteneda, A Separate Reality: Further Conversations with Don Juan (NewYork: Pocket Books, 1971) 85.

Beginning

85   Coleman Barks, trans.,The Essential Rumi (New York: Harper One, 1995), 109.

86   Shunry Suzuki, Trudy Dixon ed.,Zen Mind, Beginner's Mind (Boston, Massachusetts: Weatherhill Publications, 1974), 1.

87   Frederick Franck,trans., ChuangTzu,The Book of Angelus Silesius (Santa Fe, New Mexico: Bear and Co., Inc.),101.

88   T.S. Eliot, The Complete Poems, 1909–1950 (Orlando, Flor-
      ida: Harcourt Brace and Co., 1980), 123.

89   Johnston, W. ed. *The cloud of unknowing and The book of
      privy counselling* (New York: Image Books, 1973)

90   Cardinal Basil Hume O.S.B., Searching for God (New York:
      Ampleforth Abbey Press, 2002),? 38

91   Elizabeth Roberts and Elias Amidon ed., 365 Prayers, Bless-
      ings and Life Prayers from Around the World (San Fran-
      cisco: Tree Claude Book, Harper, 1996), 70.

92   Cardinal Basil Hume O.S.B., Searching for God (New York:
      Ampleforth Abbey Press, 2002), 153.

Choosing

93   Dietrich BonHoeffer, Geffrey B. Kelly and John D. Godsey,
      Discipleship (Minniapolis, MN., First Fortress Press, 2003),
      74.

94   Alister Clavering Hardy (Sir),The Spiritual Nature of Man:
      A Study of Contemporary Religious Experience (University
      of California: Clarendon Press, 1979), 140.

95   T.S. Eliot, The Collected Poems 1909 -1950, 209.

96   Frederick Franck, trans., The Book of Angelus Silesius, 53.

97   ————The Choice is Always Ours, 36.

98   Thomas Merton, Contemplative Prayer (New York: Image Books, 1996), 14.

99   Dorothy Berkley Phillips, The Choice is Always Ours: The Classic Anthology on the Spiritual Way (Wheaton, Il.: Theosophical Publishing House, 1974), 10.

100   Ann Marriner-Tomey and Martha Raile Alligood, Nursing Theorists and their Work, Health as Expanding Consciousness by Margaret A. Newman R.N. PhD.(Philadelphia, Pennsylvania: Mosby, 2006), 499.

Longing

101   Donald J. Moore, Martin Buber: Prophet of Religious Secularism: The Criticism of Institutional Religion in the Writings of Martin Buber (Philadelphia: Jewish Publication Society of America, 1974), 131.

102   Jonathon Kirsch, Moses: A Life (New York: Ballantine Books, 1999), 115.

103   T.S. Eliot, The Complete Poems and Plays; 1909–1950 (Orlando, Florida: Harcourt Brace and Co., 1980), 126.

104 Augustine, Confessions, trans. Henry Chadwick(Oxford: Oxford University Press, 1991), 29–30 (11.10)

105 Diane C. Randall, She of the Dreaming Sky (Atlanta, Geargia: Pearl's Book'em Publisher, 20005), 80.

106 Malcolm R. Westcott, The Psychology of Human Freedom: A Human Science Perspective and Critique (University of Michigan: Spring-Verlag, 1988), 199.

107 Rudolf Otto and John W. Harvey, The Idea of the Holy; An Inquiry into the Non-Rational Factor in the Idea of the Divine and its Relation to the Rational (Whitefish, Mont., Kessinger reprints, 2005),12.

108 Hans Urs von Balthasar, Heart of the World (San Francisco: Liturgical Press, 1979), 144.

109 Jack Kornfield, A Path with Heart: A Guide Through the Perils and Promises of the Spiritual Life (New York: Bantam Books, 1993), 154.

110 Stephen Levine, A Gradual Awakening (New York: Anchor Books, 1989.) 75.

111 J. Donald Walters, Promise of Immortality; The True Teaching of the Bible and the Bhagavad Gita (New Delhi: Sterling Publishers, 2003), 70.

112 Fulton Sheen, Life of Christ (New York: Sheed and Ward, 1958), 145.

113 Pat Rodegast and Judith Stanton, Emmanuel's Book: A Manual for Living Comfortably in the Cosmos (New York: Bantam Books, 1987), 47.

114 Sharon Salzberg, The Revolutionary Art of Happiness (Boston, Massachusetts: Shambhala Publications, 1995), 37.

115 T.S.Eliot, The Complete Poems, 1909–1950 (Orlando, Florida: Harcourt Brace and Co., 1980), 182.

Loving

116 Gordon S. Wakefield, ed. Westminster Dictionary of Christian Spirituality (Philadelphia, PA.: Westminster Press, 1983), 377.

117 Valerie Mylonas and Clifford Pia, a film, A Meeting with Emmanuel (Westport Connecticut: Friends Productions, 1990)

118 Ursula King, The Spirit of One Earth: Reflections on Teilhard de Chardin and Global Spirituality (University of Michigan: Paragon House, 1989), 179.

119 St. John of the Cross and Edgar Allison Peers, Spiritual Canticle and Poems (London: Burns and Oates, 1978), 470.

120   Thomas Merton, Counsels of Light and Love of St. John of the Cross (New York: Burns and Oates, 2007) 63.

121   Thich Nhat Hanh, The Collected Poems of Thich Nhat Hanh (Berkeley: Parallax Press, 1999), 73.

Reconciling

122   Edward Estlin Cummings, 100 Poems (New York: Grove Press, 1954)

123   Hans Urs von Balthasar, Heart of the World, 121.

124   T.S. Eliot, The Complete Poems, 1909–1950, 125–126.

125   Carlo Carretto, Letters from the Desert (Maryknoll, New York: Orbis, 1972), 120.

126   T.S. Eliot, The Complete Poems, The Cocktail Party, 146–147.

Awakening

127   Alfred Kazin,ed., The Portable Blake (New York: Penguin, 1976), 86.

128   Jack Kornfield, After the Ecstasy, The Laundry: How the Heart Grows Wise on the Spiritual Path (New York: Bantam Books, 2000), 312.

129   Homer, trans. from the Greek by Alexander Pope esq., The Iliad (Edinburgh,1769), 70.

130   Thomas Merton, Choosing to Love the World: On Contemplation (Boulder, Colorado: Sounds True Inc., 2008), 35.

131   Bernadette Roberts, The Path to No-Self: Life at the Center (Albany: State University of New York Press, 1991), 141.

132   Edward Estlin Cummings, 100 Poems (New York: Grove Press, 1954), 119.

133   Jon Kabat-Zinn Ph.D, Full Catastrophe Living: Using the Wisdom of Your Body and Mind to Face Stress, Pain, and Illness (New York: Delta Press, 1990)

134   Henry Miller, Smile at the Foot of the Ladder (New York: New Directions, 1974), 39.

135   David V. Erdman ed., The Complete Poetry and Prose of William Blake: Auguries of Innocence (New York: Anchor Books, 1988), 490.

136   Anonymous

137   Jack Kornfield and Christina Feldman,ed., Soul Food: Sto-
      ries to Nourish the Spirit and the Heart (New York: Harper
      Colllins Publishers, 1996), 232.

138   Unknown

139   Unknown

Appendix

Susan Tracy Otten, "St. Jean-Baptiste-Marie Vianney." The Catholic Encyclopedia. Vol. 8.(New York: Robert Appleton Company, 2009), 1910. <http://www.newadvent.org/cathen/08326c.htm>.

Women for Faith and Family, wf-f.org/Priests-prayer.html

Bibliography

(Sir), Alister Clavering Hardy. *The Spiritual Nature of Man: A Study of Contemporary Religious Experience.* California: Clarendon Press, 1979.

Adams, William Davenport. *Dictionary of English Literature; Being a Comprehensive Guide to English Authors and their Works.* Detroit: Gale Research Co, 1966.

Alfred Kazin, ed. *The Portable Blake.* New York: Penguin, 1976 .

Au, Wilkie. *By Way of the Heart: Toward a Holistic Spiritual Christian Spirituality.* New Jersey: Paulist Press, 1989.

Augustine, trans. Henry Chadwick. *Confessions.* Oxford: Oxford University Press, 1991.

Balthasar, Hans Urs von. *Heart of the World* . SanFrancisco: Liturgical Press, 1979.

Banks, Coleman. *The Essential Rumi* . New York: Harper One, 1995.

Barclay, William. *The Gospel of Matthew.* Kentucky: Westminster John Knox Press, 2001.

Bethune, Ade. *St. John Vianney (ABC6320).* St. Paul, Minnesota: College of St. Catherine, 1986.

Carretto, Carlo. *Letters from the Desert.* Maryknoll: Orbis, 1972. Casteneda, Carlos.

—. *A Separate Reality: Further Conversations with Don Juan.* New York: Pocket Books, 1971.

Clyde Kilby, ed. *A Mind Awake; An Anthology of C.S. Lewis Letters to Malcolm.* Florida: Harcourt C.S. Lewis, PTE Ltd., 1968.

Cummings, Edward Estlin. 100 *Poems.* New York: Grove Press, 1954.

Dietrich BonHoeffer, Geffrey B. Kelly and John D. Godsey. *Discipleship* . Minniapolis, MN: First Fortress Press, 2003.

Dillard, Annie. *Teaching a Stone to Talk: Expeditions and Encounters.* New York: Harper and Row, 1988.

Donne, John. *Time and Myth* . University of Michigan: University of Notre Dame Press, 1975.

Dunne, John. *The Reasons of the Heart: A Journey into Solitude.* New York: Macmillan, 1978.

ed, David V. Erdman. New York: Anchor Books, The Complete Poetry and Prose of William Blake: Auguries of Innocence.

ed., Elizabeth Roberts and Elias Amidon. 365 *Prayers, Blessings and Life Prayers from Around the World.* San Francisco: Tree Claude Book, Harper, 1996.

Eliot, T.S. *The Complete Poems and Plays* 1909–1950. New York: Harcourt Brace and Co., 1980.

—. *The Complete Poems and Plays* 1909–1950. Orlando: Harcourt Brace and Co, 1980 .

Gibran, Kahil. *The Prophet, 91st ed. .* New York: Alfred A. Knopf, 1973.

Gordon S. Wakefield, ed. *Westminster Dictionary of Christian Spirituality.* Philadelphia, PA: Westminster Press, 1983 .

Hanh, Thich Nhat. *Call Me by My True Names; The Collected Poems of Thich Nhat Hanh.* California: Parallax Press, 1999.

Harvey, Rudolf Otto and John W. *The Idea of the Holy; An Inquiry into the Non-Rational Factor in the Idea of the Divine and its Relation to the Rational.* Whitefish, Mont: Kessinger reprints, 2005.

Hide, Kerrie. *Gifted Origins to Graced Fulfillment: The Soteriology of Julian Norwich* . Minnesota: The Liturgical Press, 2001.

Hoff, Benjamin. *The Tao of Pooh* . New York: E.P. Dutton, 1982.

Homer, and trans. from the Greek by Alexander Pope esq. *The Iliad.* Edinburgh, 1769 .

Hume, Basil. *In Praise of Benedict.* Petersham, MA.: St. Bede's Publications, 1981.

II, Pope John Paul. , *Congregation for the Clergy L'Osservatore Romano.* www.sjbrcc.net/jp2prc.html (accessed Nov. 5, 2009).

J.L. Dawson, Peter Holland, David McKitterick. *Thomas Stearns Eliot, A Concordance to the Complete Poems and Plays of T.S. Eliot.* Neew York: Cornell University Press, 1995.

Jack Kornfield and Christina Feldman, ed. *Soul Food: Stories to Nourish the Spirit and the Heart.* New York: Harper Colllins Publishers, 1996.

John Joseph, Cardinal Carberry (+1998). *Women for Faith and Family.* 2005. www.wf-f.org (accessed October 25, 2009).

John Peter Lange D.D., Philip Schaff D.D., ed., Volume 5. *A Commentary on the Holy Scriptures* . New York: Scribners, 1877.

Johnston, W. ed. *The cloud of unknowing and The book of privy counselling.* New York: Image Books, 1973.

Karl Rahner, trans. and foreword by James M. Demske, SJ. *Encounters with Silence* . South Bend, Indiana: St. Augustine's Press, 1999.

King, Ursula. *The Spirit of One Earth: Reflections on Teilhard de Chardin and Global Spirituality.* University of Michigan: Paragon House, 1989.

Kirsch, Jonathon. *Moses: A Life.* New York: Ballantine Books, 1999.

Kornfield, Jack. *A Path with Heart: A Guide Through the Perils and Promises of the Spiritual Life.* New York: Bantam Books, 1993 .

—. *After the Ecstasy, The Laundry: How the Heart Grows Wise on the Spiritual Path* . New York: Bantam Books, 2000.

—. "Dharma Talk." Barre, December 1981.

—. *The Wise Heart.* New York: Bantam, 2009.

L'Engle, Madeleine. *Walking on Water; Reflections on Faith and Art* . New York: North Point Press, 1980.

LaFemina, Msgr. Anthony. *Voices Online Edition, Vol. XVIII: No. 2, Vocations Issue.* Pentecost 2003. www.wf-f.org. (accessed November 9, 2009).

Lao Tsu and Gia-Fu Fing, Jane Enlish (trans.). *Tao te Ching.* New York: Knopf Doubleday Group, 1989.

Levine, Stephen. *A Gradual Awakening.* New York: Anchor Books, 1989 .

Lewis, C.S. *The Four Loves* . New York: Harcourt Books, 1968.

Looy, H.vander. *Rule for a New Brother* . Springfield Illinois: Templegate Publishers, 1976.

Lucado, Max. *Meet the God of Encouragement, Multnomah Books, ch.* 2. 1994. www.maxlucado.com/articles/topical/me (accessed October 15, 2009).

McCarthy, Coleman. *Inner Companions* . California: Acropolis, 1975.

McCarthy, Colman. *Inner Companions* . Calif.: Acropolis, 1975.

McDonald, Michele. "Dharma Talk." Barre, June 9, 2008, 2009.

Merton, Thomas. *Thoughts in Solitude* . New York: Farrar,Strauss, and Giroux, 1999.

—. *Counsels of Light and Love of St. John of the Cross.* New York: Burns and Oates, 2007.

—. *On Contemplation, Choosing to Love the World.* Boulder, Colorado: Sounds True Inc, 2008 .

Miller, Henry. *Smile at the Foot of the Ladder.* New York: New Directions, 1974.

Moore, Donald J. *Martin Buber: Prophet of Religious Secularism: The Criticism of Institutional Religion in the Writings of Martin Bube.* Philadelphia: Jewish Publication Society of America, 1974 .

New American Standard Bible . La Habra: The Lockman Foundation, 1995.

Newman, John Henry. *Sermon 1: The Philosophical Temper First Enjoyed by the Gospel, Oxford University National Institute for Newman Studies* . 1826. www.newmanreader.org/works/oxford/sermon (accessed October 10, 2009).

Nouwen, Henri. *Life of the Beloved; Spiritual Living in a Secular World.* New York: Crossroad Publishing Co., 1992.

—. *Clowning in Rome.* New York: Image Books, Doubleday, 1979.

—. *The Wounded Healer, Ministry in Contemporary Society* . New York: Doubleday, 1972.

O.S.B., Cardinal Basil Hume. *Searching for God.* New York: Ampleforth Abbey Press, 2002.

P.Hall, Gary. *Autonomy and Surrender; Solitude and Intimacy.* www.thomasmertonsociety.org/hall.htm (accessed November 2, 2009).

Padovano, Anthony. *Free to be Faithful* . Paramus, New Jersey: Paulist Press, 1972.

Pease, Glenn. *Matthew 17: 1–13: Commentary. When the Son Glowed like the Sun, Chapter 4: 1.* www.scribd.com/doc/21345199/ (accessed October 20, 2009).

Peck, Michael Scott. *The Road Less Traveled and Beyond Spiritual Growth in an Age of Anxiety.* New York: Touchstone, 1998.

Peers, St. John of the Cross and Edgar Allison. *Spiritual Canticle and Poems.* London: Burns and Oates, 1978 .

Ph.D, Jon Kabat-Zinn. *Full Catastrophe Living: Using the Wisdom of Your Body and Mind to Face Stress, Pain, and Illness.* New York: Delta Press, 1991.

PhD, Margaret A. Newman R.N.Ann Marriner-Tomey and Martha Raile Alligood. *Nursing Theorists and their Work, Health as Expanding Consciousness .* Philadelphia, Pennsylvania: Mosby, 2006.

Phillips, Dorothy Berkley. *The Choice is Always Ours.* University of California: Re-quest Books, 1982.

Pia, Valerie Mylonas and Clifford. *A Meeting with Emmanuel; a film.* Westport Connecticut: Friends Productions, 1990.

Plato, trans. .by G.M. Grube. *The Republic .* Indiannapolis, Indiana: Hackett, 1992 .

Randall, Diane C. *She of the Dreaming Sky.* Atlanta, Geargia: Pearl's Book'em Publisher, 2005.

Roberts, Bernadette. *The Path to No-Self: Life at the Center.* Albany: State University of New York Press, 1991.

Rowan Williams, Desmond Tutu and Lawrence Freeman. *Where GoHappens; Discovering God in One Another.* Boston, Massachusetts: New Seeds Books, 2005.

Russell, Bertrand. *History of Western Philosophy.* Bulwell Lane, Basford: Bertrand Russell Peace Foundation, 1996.

Ryan, Thomas. *Prayer of Heart and Body: Meditation and Yoga as Christian Spiritual Practice.* New York: The Missionary Society of St. Paul the Apostle, 1995.

Salzberg, Sharon. *The Revolutionary Art of Happiness* . Boston, Massachusetts: Shambhala Publications, 1995.

Sheen, I. Fulton. *Life of Christ.* New York: Sheed and Ward, 1958.

Short, Robert L. *The Gospel According to Peanuts* . Kentucky: Westminster John Knox Press, 2003.

Shunry Suzuki, Trudy Dixon ed. *Zen Mind, Beginner's Mind* . Boston: Weatherhill Publications, 1974.

Silverstein, Shel. *The Giving Tree; Lafcadio, The Lion Who Shot Back.* New York: Harper Collins, 1992.

Snell, Rainer Maria Rilke and Reginald. *Letters to a Young Poet* . New York: Dover Publications, 2002.

—. *Letters to a Young Poet.* New York: Dover Publications, 2002.

Stanton, Pat Rodegast and Judith. *Emmanuel's Book: A Manual for Living Comfortably in the Cosmos.* New York: Bantam Books, 1987.

Susan Tracy Otten, "St. Jean-Baptiste-Marie Vianney." The Catholic Encyclopedia. Vol. 8.(New York: Robert Appleton C ompany. *New Advent.* 2009. <http://www.newadvent.org/cathen/08326c.htm> (accessed October 25, 2009).

Teresa, Mother. *Words to Love By.* Indiana: Ave Maria Press, 1985.

The Real Meaning of Life and Human Existence. 2004. www.new-age-spirituality.com/meanlife.html (accessed October 6, 2009).

Thomas Merton, M. Basil Pennington. *Thomas Merton; I Have Seen What I Was Looking For: Selected Spiritual Writings.* New York: New City Press, 2005.

—. *Thomas Merton; I Have Seen What I Was Looking For: Selected Spiritual Writings.* New York: New City Press, 2005.

Tozer, A.W. *The Pursuit of God; Finding the Divine in the Everyday.* Peabody, MA.: Christian Publications, 1993.

Walters, J. Donald. *Promise of Immortality; The True Teaching of the Bible and the Bhagavad Gita.* New Delhi: Sterling Publishers, 2003.

Westcott, Malcolm R. *The Psychology of Human Freedom: A Human Science Perspective and Critique* . University of Michigan: Spring-Verlag, 1988.

Wilde, Oscar. *The Complete Works of Oscar Wilde, Volume 8.* New York: National Library, 1909.